ECDL® 5.0

European Computer Driving Licence

Module 6 - Presentation

using PowerPoint 2007

This training, which has been approved by ECDL Foundation, includes exercise items intended to assist Candidates in their training for an ECDL Certification Programme. These exercises are not ECDL Foundation certification tests. For information about authorised Test Centres in different national territories, please refer to the ECDL Foundation website at www.ecdl.org

Release ECDL253v1

Published by:

       CiA Training Ltd
       Business & Innovation Centre
       Sunderland Enterprise Park
       Sunderland SR5 2TA
       United Kingdom

       Tel: +44 (0) 191 549 5002
       Fax: +44 (0) 191 549 9005

       E-mail: info@ciatraining.co.uk
       Web: www.ciatraining.co.uk

       ISBN-13: 978 1 86005 679 6

The following information applies <u>only</u> to candidates in Ireland.

Acknowledgements:

The European Computer Driving Licence is operated in Ireland by ICS Skills, the training and certification body of the Irish Computer Society.
Candidates using this courseware should register online with ICS Skills through an approved ECDL Test Centre. Without a valid registration, and the allocation of a unique ICS Skills ID number or SkillsCard, no ECDL tests can be taken and no certificate, or any other form of recognition, can be given to a candidate.

Other ECDL Foundation Certification programmes offered by ICS Skills include Equalskills, ECDL Advanced, ECDL WebStarter, ECDL ImageMaker, EUCIP and Certified Training Professional.

Contact: ICS Skills
              Crescent Hall
              Mount Street Crescent
              Dublin 2
              Ireland

Website: www.ics.ie/skills

Email: *skills@ics.ie*

First published 2008

European Computer Driving Licence, ECDL, International Computer Driving Licence, ICDL, e-Citizen and related logos are all registered Trade Marks of The European Computer Driving Licence Foundation Limited ("ECDL Foundation").

CiA Training Ltd is an entity independent of ECDL Foundation and is not associated with ECDL Foundation in any manner. This courseware may be used to assist candidates to prepare for the ECDL Foundation Certification Programme as titled on the courseware. Neither ECDL Foundation nor **CiA Training Ltd** warrants that the use of this courseware publication will ensure passing of the tests for that ECDL Foundation Certification Programme. This courseware publication has been independently reviewed and approved by ECDL Foundation as covering the learning objectives for the ECDL Foundation Certification Programme.

Confirmation of this approval can be obtained by reviewing the Partners Page in the About Us Section of the website www.ecdl.org

The material contained in this courseware publication has not been reviewed for technical accuracy and does not guarantee that candidates will pass the test for the ECDL Foundation Certification Programme. Any and all assessment items and/or performance-based exercises contained in this courseware relate solely to this publication and do not constitute or imply certification by ECDL Foundation in respect of the ECDL Foundation Certification Programme or any other ECDL Foundation test. Irrespective of how the material contained in this courseware is deployed, for example in a learning management system (LMS) or a customised interface, nothing should suggest to the candidate that this material constitutes certification or can lead to certification through any other process than official ECDL Foundation certification testing.

For details on sitting a test for an ECDL Foundation certification programme, please contact your country's designated National Licensee or visit the ECDL Foundation's website at www.ecdl.org.

Candidates using this courseware must be registered with the National Operator before undertaking a test for an ECDL Foundation Certification Programme. Without a valid registration, the test(s) cannot be undertaken and no certificate, nor any other form of recognition, can be given to a candidate. Registration should be undertaken with your country's designated National Licensee at an Approved Test Centre.

ECDL Foundation
Approved Courseware

Class: 00 4h5 ECDL

Accession No: ECDL |2011>

Type: 3 week

Downloading the Data Files

The data associated with these exercises must be downloaded from our website. Go to: *www.ciatraining.co.uk/data*. Follow the on screen instructions to download the appropriate data files.

By default, the data files will be downloaded to **Documents\CIA DATA FILES\ECDL\6 Presentations** (Note: *Windows XP* downloads to a **My Documents** folder).

If you prefer, the data can be supplied on CD at an additional cost. Contact the Sales team at *info@ciatraining.co.uk*.

Aims

To demonstrate the ability to use a presentation application on a personal computer.

To understand and accomplish basic operations associated with *PowerPoint*.

Objectives

After completing the guide the user will be able to:

- Work with presentations and save them in different file formats

- Choose built in options such as the Help function within the application to enhance productivity

- Understand different presentation views and when to use them, choose different slide layouts and designs and edit slides

- Enter, edit and format text in presentations. Recognise good practice in applying unique titles to slides

- Choose, create and format charts to communicate information meaningfully

- Insert and edit pictures, images and drawn objects

- Apply animation and transition effects to presentations and check and correct presentation content before finally printing and giving presentations.

Assessment of Knowledge

At the end of this guide is a section called the **Record of Achievement Matrix**. Before the guide is started it is recommended that the user complete the matrix to measure the level of current knowledge.

Tick boxes are provided for each feature. **1** is for no knowledge, **2** some knowledge and **3** is for competent.

After working through a section, complete the **Record of Achievement** matrix for that section and only when competent in all areas move on to the next section.

Contents

Section 1
Getting Started

By the end of this Section you should be able to:

Understand *PowerPoint* Principles

Start *PowerPoint*

Use an Installed Template

Recognise the Screen Layout

Understand the Ribbon and Quick Access Toolbar

Use Help

Change Preferences

Exit *PowerPoint*

To gain an understanding of the above features, work through the **Driving Lessons** in this **Section**.

For each **Driving Lesson**, read the **Park and Read** instructions, without touching the keyboard, then work through the numbered steps of the **Manoeuvres** on the computer. Complete the **Revision Exercise(s)** at the end of the section to test your knowledge.

Driving Lesson 1 - Starting PowerPoint

▣ Park and Read

PowerPoint allows complicated and impressive presentations to be produced with ease.

The presentations can be used for on-screen shows, overhead projector shows, producing 35mm slides or for creating presentations and Web pages for use on the Internet.

They can include text in any format, pictures, organisation charts, graphs, sound and film clips, and information from the Internet. The slide show can incorporate impressive text animation and slide effects.

As well as slides, *PowerPoint* can produce presentation notes, handouts, printouts of slides and outlines of text.

There are numerous ways to start the program. The following method is recommended for beginners.

Manoeuvres

1.   Starting the computer will automatically show the *Windows* **Desktop**.

2.   Click once on [icon] to show the **Start** menu. All *Windows* applications can be started here.

3.   Move the mouse pointer over **All Programs**. Click the | Microsoft Office | folder and then | Microsoft Office PowerPoint 2007 |.

ℹ️ *If PowerPoint has been used recently there may be an entry for it in the **Start** menu and it can be started from there.*

4.   If the **Tip of the Day** dialog box appears, click on **Close**.

5.   The opening *PowerPoint* screen is displayed. Leave the blank presentation open for the next Driving Lesson.

ℹ️ *To close PowerPoint click on the **Office Button**, [icon], and then select **Exit PowerPoint**, | X Exit PowerPoint |.*

Driving Lesson 2 - The PowerPoint Screen

▣ Park and Read

Title Bar

Office Button

Ribbon Tabs

Ribbon Groups

Slides/Outline Pane

Click to add title

Click to add subtitle

Slide Pane

Notes Pane

Status Bar

Click to add notes

The screen should be similar to the above diagram. Work through the following manoeuvres to locate the features.

⟰ Manoeuvres

1. Look at the top line, the **Title Bar**, displaying **Microsoft PowerPoint**. It also shows the title of the current presentation.

2. Below that is the **Ribbon**, where commands are chosen using the mouse. It is made up of **Tabs** (the words at the top of the ribbon, which illuminate when the mouse is rolled over them), **Groups** (the boxes which spread horizontally across the ribbon, distinguishable by their names at the bottom of each) and **Commands** (the icons within groups which perform different actions).

3. Find the bar at the bottom of the screen. This is called the **Status Bar**, where the slide number and template design will be displayed.

4. The main part of the screen shows various views of the current presentation. The default view, shown here is **Normal** view.

5. In the top left corner of the screen, click the **Office Button**, [icon], and select **New**. This dialog box deals with opening and creating a new presentation.

6. Click [X] to close the **New Presentation** dialog box.

Driving Lesson 3 - Presentations

▣ Park and Read

The *PowerPoint* **New Presentation** dialog box offers various ways to start a new presentation.

Templates allow the basic background design to be chosen from any previously saved templates. Individual slides and content can then be created with this background already applied.

Microsoft Office Online allows users to choose from hundreds of online templates. An internet connection is required to access these files.

Blank and recent presentation provides no preset options. The user defines the layout, content and background for all slides. **Themes** can be applied later.

Recently Used Templates allows the basic background design to be chosen from any templates which have been used or modified recently (none may be shown when the application is started for the first time. This can allow quicker access for users who have paused whilst planning or designing a presentation.

⌒ Manoeuvres

1. Click the **Microsoft Office Button**, and select **New**.

2. Click **Installed Templates**, and from the gallery double click **Introducing PowerPoint 2007**.

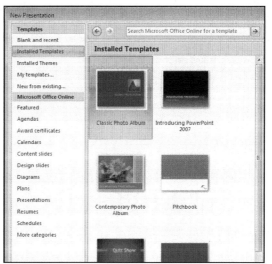

3. Notice the three distinct areas of the screen. At the left is a slim panel which displays either **Slides** or **Outline**. Make sure the **Slides** tab is selected.

4. This template is complete with a number of slides designed to demonstrate the benefits of *Microsoft PowerPoint 2007*. However, you can now add and remove slides and modify the contents as required.

5. Keep this presentation on screen for the next few Driving Lessons.

Driving Lesson 4 - The Ribbon

▣ Park and Read

In previous versions of *Microsoft Office* applications, commands were controlled by a series of menus and toolbars. *PowerPoint 2007* has replaced these with a **Ribbon** which is displayed at the top of the application window. The **Ribbon** contains buttons and drop down lists to control the operation of *PowerPoint*. The **Ribbon** is divided into a series of **Tabs**, each of which has a set of controls specific to a certain function or process. On each tab, the controls are further divided into separate **Groups** of connected functions.

Some tabs can be selected manually, some only appear when certain operations are active, for example only when a **Chart** is active, will **Chart Tools** tabs be displayed on the **Ribbon**.

Above the **Ribbon** is the **Quick Access Toolbar** which contains a few popular command buttons. By default this toolbar has three buttons, **Save**, **Undo** and **Repeat**. This toolbar can be customised by adding further buttons.

⌇ Manoeuvres

1.   On the **Ribbon**, the **Home** tab should be selected. Other basic tabs are available.

☒ *The **Ribbon** can be minimized by right clicking anywhere on it, then from the drop down list, select **Minimize the Ribbon**. To undo this, simply repeat the process but de-select **Minimize the Ribbon**.*

*Part of the **Ribbon** displaying the **Home** tab*

☒ *Any buttons or commands displayed in pale grey are called **ghosted** and are not available to be selected at present.*

2.   Notice how the buttons on the **Ribbon** are divided into **Groups** (**Clipboard**, **Slides**, **Font**, etc.).

☒ *The display of buttons on the **Ribbon** is dynamic. That is it will change according to how much space there is available. If the window is not maximised or the screen resolution is anything other than 1024 by 768, the **Ribbon** will not always appear as shown in this guide.*

Driving Lesson 4 - Continued

3. Leave the cursor over of any the buttons. A **ToolTip** appears which give more information and an alternative key press for the function if available.

> Italic (Ctrl+I)
>
> Italicize the selected text.

4. Some buttons produce immediate effects, like the **Bold**, **Italic** and **Underline** buttons in the **Font** group.

5. Buttons with a drop down arrow lead to further options. Click the **Shapes** button, which is found in the **Drawing** group. A list of further options is displayed. Click the button again to remove the options.

6. Some options will display a dialog box which needs data to be entered. Click the **Replace** button, the **Replace** dialog box is displayed, where text can be found or replaced. Click the **Close** button in the dialog box to remove it.

7. Some groups have a dialog box launcher to the right of the group name, e.g. the **Font** group, `Font`

8. Click on the word **Introducing** in the main slide, click the **Font** dialog box launcher to display the **Font** dialog box.

9. This is a tabbed dialog box, showing the current format of the selected word. Click **Cancel** to close the **Font** dialog box.

10. Display the other basic tabs, one at a time, **Insert**, **Design**, **Animations**, **Slide Show**, **Review** and **View** to see which other commands are available. The **Drawing Tools**, **Format** tab will also be displayed, if the insertion point is still within the word **Introducing**.

11. Select the **Home** tab again.

Driving Lesson 5 - The Quick Access Toolbar

▣ Park and Read

Above the **Ribbon** is the **Quick Access Toolbar** which contains a few popular command buttons. By default this toolbar has three buttons, **Save**, **Undo** and **Repeat**. This toolbar can be customised by adding further buttons.

〽 Manoeuvres

1.   Locate the **Quick Access Toolbar**.

2.   Point at each button on the **Quick Access Toolbar** and read its **ToolTip**.

3.   The third button is the **Repeat** button. This button has a dual function, it changes to a **Redo** button after the **Undo** button has been used.

4.   To the right of the **Repeat** button is the **Customize Quick Access Toolbar** button, ▾. Click the button to display the menu.

Customize Quick Access Toolbar
New
Open
√ Save
E-mail
Quick Print
Print Preview
Spelling
√ Undo
√ Redo
Slide Show From Beginning
More Commands...
Show Below the Ribbon
Minimize the Ribbon

5.   To add commands not shown, click **More Commands**. This displays the **PowerPoint Options** window with the **Customize** option selected. This window is covered later in the **Preferences** exercise.

6.   Click **Cancel** to close the window.

Driving Lesson 6 - Help

▣ Park and Read

PowerPoint has a comprehensive **Help** facility. This means that full advantage can be taken of the features incorporated in the program. Using **Help** can usually solve the majority of problems encountered.

Help topics are available either from **Microsoft Office Online** via the internet, or from the content installed on your computer (**Offline**). The method of using **Help** is the same in either case but the content may vary slightly and there will be some extra options when online. This guide assumes the **Online** option is selected.

⌁ Manoeuvres

1. Click the **Help** button, ⬤ in the upper right corner of the *PowerPoint* window to display the **PowerPoint Help** window. If the **Table of Contents** is not displayed on the left, click ◉ .

  *Pressing the <F1> key will display the same **Help** window. The window can be moved, resized or maximised if required.*

![PowerPoint Help window screenshot showing the Table of Contents on the left and Browse PowerPoint Help topics on the right]

Driving Lesson 6 - Continued

2. **Help** can be used in two ways: either type in keywords into the **Search** box or browse through the listed topics.

3. Type **printer** into the **Search** box and click, [🔍 Search ▾]. There will be many topics found for your search and it will be necessary to locate the most appropriate.

4. Click the topic **Set the default printer**. Help text for this topic is displayed.

5. Read the text then click the **Back** button, [⬅], on the dialog box toolbar to return to the previous screen. Click **Back** again to return to the main help screen.

6. Type **"delete slide"** into the **Search** box and click, [🔍 Search ▾]. The quotation marks force the whole phrase to be used and may help to narrow down the search.

7. Click the first topic in the list. Help text for this topic is displayed.

8. Read the text then click the **Home** button, [🏠], on the dialog box toolbar to return directly to the original help screen.

9. Type **xyz** into the **Search** box and click, [🔍 Search ▾]. As the text is not found, some suggestions are made to help you find the required information. There are more options when connected online.

10. Click the **Home** button, [🏠], to return directly to the original help screen.

11. On the home screen, all available help topics are grouped into a list of categories. The list is shown in the **Table of Contents** on the left and again in two columns in the main display area Click on the **Creating a presentation** category from either list. A list of topics for this heading is displayed. There are two further subcategories which could be expanded.

12. Click **Fonts and formatting**. A list of **Topics** is displayed.

13. Click on a topic and **Help** on the topic is displayed. Scroll down the help. There may be links to other related topics.

14. Click the **Home** button, [🏠].

[ℹ️] *The **Table of Contents** can be hidden by clicking the* [📖] *button.*

15. The button at the bottom right of the window indicates whether you are connected to **Office Online** or not (**Offline**). Click on the button to see the available options. Click in the **Help** window to remove the options.

16. Close the **Help** window, by clicking its **Close** button, [✖].

Driving Lesson 7 - Preferences

▣ Park and Read

Basic options (**preferences**) can be changed in *PowerPoint;* for example, the default save directory. By default, documents are opened from and saved to the **Documents** folder. This location can be changed. It is also possible to change the user name. By default, the person who installed the application is named as the user. It can be changed to show a different name, which will then appear on presentations created from templates.

☞ Manoeuvres

1. Click the **Office Button**, , then select **Open** and notice that the save location box in the **Open** dialog box shows **Documents**.

2. Click **Cancel** to close the dialog box and click ▣. The **Save As** dialog box also saves by default to **Documents.**

3. To change this file location, click **Cancel** to close the dialog box, then click the **Office Button** and click ⟦ PowerPoint Options ⟧.

4. Click **Save** at the left of the **PowerPoint Options** dialog box.

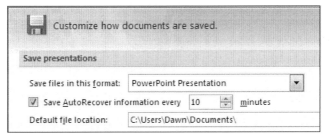

5. In the **Default file location** box, click at the end of the existing text and add **CIA DATA FILES\ECDL\6 Presentations**. Click **OK**.

6. Click the **Save** button, ▣, on the **Quick Access Toolbar** and notice that the new location is shown.

Driving Lesson 7 - Continued

7. Cancel the dialog box. To change the settings back, display the **PowerPoint Options** dialog box and the **Save** options. In the **Default file location** box, amend the entry by deleting **CIA DATA FILES\ECDL 2007\6 Presentations**, so that the location ends with **Documents** and click **OK**.

8. Display **PowerPoint Options** again and select the **Popular** button from the dialog box.

9. Under the heading **Personalize your copy of Microsoft Office**, delete any existing information and enter your own details. This changes the **User Information** associated with the presentation.

10. Click **OK** to apply the new settings.

11. The changed settings will only be used for new presentations.

12. Start a new presentation by clicking the **Office Button** , **New** then **Create**.

13. To check the user name click the **Office Button**, place the cursor over **Prepare** and click **Properties** at the top right of the menu.

14. The **Document Properties** window is displayed. Check your name as **Author** and then close the window by clicking the **Close** button at the right of the **Document Properties** window.

15. Close the presentation, using the **Office Button** and **Close**.

16. Leave *PowerPoint* open for the next exercise.

Driving Lesson 8 - Closing PowerPoint

▣ Park and Read

PowerPoint can be closed in a number of different ways, all of which are accessible from within the *PowerPoint* screen. Choose one of the following ways to close the program.

⌔ Manoeuvres

1. Click the **Office Button** and then ╳ Exit PowerPoint , at the bottom right of the menu, to close *PowerPoint*. As no changes have been made, and only one presentation is open, *PowerPoint* closes.

| i | *If changes have been made to a recently saved presentation, or a new presentation created since the last save, a dialog box is displayed upon trying to exit the program (as shown below).*

| i | *Clicking **Yes** would start the Save process, which is covered in the next section, and then close PowerPoint. Clicking **No** would close PowerPoint without saving anything. Clicking **Cancel**, would cancel the close process and return to the PowerPoint window.*

2. Reopen *PowerPoint*.

3. Click the **Close** button ▣ on the **Title Bar** (black bar) at the top-right corner of the screen. Again, no changes were made so no saving options are given.

| i | *Normally when closing PowerPoint with either of these actions, the **Yes** option will be taken to ensure that any important information is saved. All unsaved data will be permanently lost. Saving will be covered later.*

| i | *Another method that can be used to close PowerPoint down is the key press <**Alt F4**>.*

Driving Lesson 9 - Revision

This covers the features introduced in this section. Try not to refer to the preceding Driving Lessons while completing it.

1.　Start *PowerPoint*.

2.　What are the options available from the **New Presentation** dialog box for creating a new presentation?

3.　How many buttons are displayed on the **Quick Access Toolbar**?

4.　Use the **ToolTips** on the buttons to find what they are?

5.　What does it mean if a button is ghosted?

6.　What is the **Ribbon**?

7.　The **Ribbon** tabs are **Home**, **View**, **Animations**, **Insert**, **Slide Show**, **Design** and which other? (the **Developer** tab may be listed but this is not displayed by default).

8.　List the presentations available from the **Installed Templates** category.

9.　What are **Preferences**?

10.　Display the **New Presentation** dialog box and select **Installed Templates**.

11.　Open the **Quiz Show** presentation and display the **Insert** tab.

12.　Use **ToolTips** to discover the functions of the buttons.

13.　Redisplay the **Home** tab.

14.　Using **Help** to search for information on previewing animations.

15.　Find information on **Creating a presentation**.

16.　Select **Create a basic presentation in PowerPoint 2007** and read the instructions.

17.　Close the **PowerPoint Help** window.

18.　Display the **Slide Show** tab.

19.　How many groups are shown?

20.　Exit *PowerPoint*.

i *Answers to this revision exercise can be found at the end of this guide.*

If you experienced any difficulty completing the Revision, refer back to the Driving Lessons in this section. Then redo the Revision.

Driving Lesson 10 - Revision

This covers the features introduced in this section. Try not to refer to the preceding Driving Lessons while completing it.

1. Start *PowerPoint*.

2. Use **PowerPoint Options** to change your **User Name** to **Charles Dickens**.

3. Use the **Installed Templates** to create a **Contemporary Photo Album** presentation.

4. Use **ToolTips** to discover the functions of the following buttons:

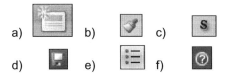

5. Use **PowerPoint Options** to change your **User Name** back to your name.

6. Exit *PowerPoint*.

7. Start PowerPoint.

8. Use the **Installed Templates** to open a **Widescreen Presentation**.

9. View the **Drawing** group on the **Home** tab.

10. View the **Illustrations** group on the **Insert** tab.

11. Use **Microsoft Office PowerPoint Help** to search for information about **Notes**.

12. Use the search bar to find out how to change the slide background, by entering **slide background**. Click on **Add a background to your presentation** and select **Add a background style to your presentation** from the **Help** window.

13. Close the **Help** window.

14. Close *PowerPoint* without saving.

i *Answers to this revision exercise can be found at the end of this guide.*

If you experienced any difficulty completing the Revision, refer back to the Driving Lessons in this section. Then redo the Revision.

Once you are confident with the features, complete the Record of Achievement Matrix referring to the section at the end of the guide. Only when competent move on to the next Section.

Section 2
Slides & Presentations

By the end of this Section you should be able to:

Understand and Use Different Views

Understand Slide Show Basics

Save, Close and Open Presentations

Use Presentation / Design Templates

Create a Blank Presentation

Add New Slides / Insert Slides / Delete Slides

Change Slide Layout and Background

To gain an understanding of the above features, work through the **Driving Lessons** in this **Section**.

For each **Driving Lesson**, read the **Park and Read** instructions, without touching the keyboard, then work through the numbered steps of the **Manoeuvres** on the computer. Complete the **Revision Exercise(s)** at the end of the section to test your knowledge.

Driving Lesson 11 - Views

▣ Park and Read

The *PowerPoint* **View** menu lists four different ways to view a presentation on screen. Each view shows a different aspect of the presentation. The views are:

Normal		Combines the main **Slide** view with an **Outline** view, a multiple **Slides** view and an area for **Notes**. Each area of the screen can be resized individually.
Slide Sorter		A miniature of each slide is shown. Used to order slides, add transition and animation effects (covered in later Driving Lessons).
Slide Show		Used to view presentations.
Notes Page		Used to create presenter's notes for the slides (only available from **View** menu).

Quick access buttons for the first three of these views are found at the lower right of most *PowerPoint* screens.

Views within the **Normal** view are:

Slide view — Used to change the text, graphics and layout of a slide and to add graphics and artwork from other applications. One slide is viewed at a time.

Outline view — Used to add or edit the presentation page titles and text. The information is shown as text only.

Slides view — List of miniature slide images with the same functions as **Slide Sorter** view. Occupies the same pane as **Outline** view, tabs are used to toggle between them.

☞ Manoeuvres

1. Start *PowerPoint*. Click the **Office Button** and select **New**.

2. From the **New Presentation** dialog box, select **Installed Templates**. Select **Introducing PowerPoint 2007** and click **Create**.

3. Click on the **View** tab. **Normal** view is displayed by default. Click the **Slide Sorter** view button, . Several slides of the presentation are shown on the screen at once.

Driving Lesson 11 - Continued

4.   Click on the **Notes Page** button. The slide is shown in the top of the screen, with an area for notes at the bottom.

5.   Click the **Slide Show** button, at the bottom right of the screen. The presentation slide show starts, beginning with the currently viewed slide.

6.   Click the mouse button to go from one slide to the next. Each page is shown in turn on the screen. Continue to the end or press <**Esc**> to finish.

7.   Make sure **Normal** view, is selected and click on the **Slides** tab, **Slides Outline**. A list of slide miniatures is displayed with the current slide (as shown in the **Slide** pane) highlighted.

8.   Each pane works independently of the others, although they are also linked. Click slide **4** in the **Slides** list and slide **4** will be shown in the **Slide** pane. Click in the **Slide** pane.

9.   Display the **View** tab, click **Zoom** and choose **100%** from the **Zoom** dialog box. Click **OK**.

10. Use the scroll bar at the bottom of the **Slide** pane to see more of the slide.

11. Now click **Zoom** again and select **Fit** from the list. Click **OK**. The slide returns to its dimensions when *PowerPoint* was originally opened.

12. Select the **Outline** tab, **Slides Outline** to show the contents of the slides in the left pane. Each slide is represented by a small icon and the slide number, 1.

13. Use the scroll bar at the right of the pane to display slide **12**. Move the mouse over the icon until it becomes 12. Click once to display slide **12** in the **Slide** pane. The associated text and icon are highlighted in the **Outline** pane.

14. Move the mouse over the border at the right of the **Outline** pane until it becomes. Click and drag to change the size of the pane until it fills about half the screen. Drag to the left to decrease the size of the pane or to the right to increase it. Drag the border back to its original position.

15. View slide **15**, **Quick Styles**. Click in the **Notes** pane (Click to add notes) and type in **Mention the huge number available**.

16. Switch back to **Slides** view and practise moving between slides. Leave the presentation on screen for the next Driving Lesson.

Driving Lesson 12 - Slide View

▣ Park and Read

Slide View - this is shown in the pane at the right within **Normal** view - it shows the presentation slides, one at a time, with all text properly formatted and with a background template. This is the main area used to create, edit and format most slide content.

The scroll bar at the right of the screen can be used to move from one slide to another.

In all the views except **Slide Show**, pressing <**Ctrl Home**> or <**Ctrl End**> moves directly to the first or last slide in a presentation respectively.

⤴ Manoeuvres

1.   The presentation created earlier should still be on screen.

2.   Click on slide **7**.

3.   Click on the **Next Slide** button, ⬇, to move to the next slide.

4.   Click on the **Previous Slide** button, ⬆, to move back one slide.

5.   Click and drag the scroll button up or down the scroll bar, as appropriate. Release the mouse button when the marker for slide **14**, **Mix It Up**, appears.

> Slide: 14 of 18
> Mix It Up!

6.   Press <**Ctrl End**> to move to the last slide in the presentation.

7.   Press <**Ctrl Home**> to move to the first slide in the presentation.

8.   Practise moving through the slides in **Normal** view, then return to **Slide 1**.

Driving Lesson 13 - Slides and Outline View

▣ Park and Read

Slides and **Outline** views are optional within **Normal** view. Either can be used to move to different slides or rearrange slides in the context of the presentation.

Slides view does this using thumbnail pictures, while **Outline** uses only text. Text can be entered in **Outline** view and it will appear on the slide. Text can also be hidden in **Outline** view so that only the slide titles appear. This is useful if there are a number of slides which need to be reordered.

If the pane using these options is narrowed, then the tab titles are replaced with pictures.

⌂ Manoeuvres

1.   With the **Introducing PowerPoint** presentation still on screen, from within the **Slides** tab, click on slide **3 Text Graphics & Pictures**.

2.   The slide is shown in the main part of the window.

3.   Move the scroll button in the **Slides** tab down so that slide **9** is in view.

4.   Click on it. It is now on view in the **Slide** pane.

5.   Click on the **Outline** tab. The pane expands to better accommodate the text. Note that no graphics appear in outline view.

6.   The current slide is shown as ▦. There is no text in the view for this slide because the text on the slide is actually part of the graphic.

7.   Click on slide **12**. The slide title and text becomes highlighted in **Outline**.

☞

Driving Lesson 13 - Continued

8.   In the **Outline** pane, click at the end of the text for slide **12**, beyond the highlighted text. The flashing insertion point cursor should be shown.

9.   Press <**Enter**> and type the text: **Text can be added in Outline view**. The text appears on the slide.

10.   Double click on the slide icon for slide 12. The slide text is hidden; only the title is shown, underlined, to denote the hidden words.

11.   Right click anywhere in the **Outline** pane and select **Collapse | Collapse All**. All text apart from the slide headings is hidden.

12.   Right click anywhere in the **Outline** pane and select **Expand | Expand All**. All text is now shown again.

13.   Click on the **Slides** tab.

14.   Close the **Slides/Outline** pane by clicking on 🗙, this gives more space to the slide.

15.   Click the **View** tab and then **Normal** view button 🔲, to replace the **Slides** pane on screen.

Driving Lesson 14 - Slide Sorter View

▣ Park and Read

Slide Sorter View shows a thumbnail of slides in a presentation on screen. This makes it easy to move, add or delete slides and to decide on animated transitions (special effects, e.g. fade or dissolve) for moving from slide to slide. Transitions and effects are covered in later Driving Lessons.

ℳ Manoeuvres

1. With the presentation still on screen, switch to **Slide Sorter** view. The screen will appear similar to below. Use the **Zoom Control** slider on the **Status bar**, [66% ⊖———⊕], to display more or fewer slides (fewer slides will be shown if the screen resolution is below 1024x768).

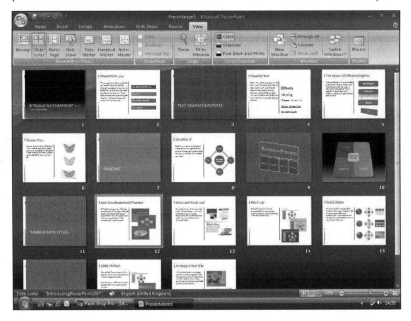

2. Click on the middle of slide number **3**, hold down the left mouse button and move it about the screen. Notice that as the mouse pointer moves about the screen, an orange line appears, moving between slides. When the mouse button is released, the line is replaced by the slide.

3. Release the mouse button when the line is to the left of slide **6**. The **Text, Graphics & Pictures** slide has now become slide **5**.

Driving Lesson 15 - Notes Page View

▣ Park and Read

Notes Page view allows presenter's notes to be added to slides. The top of the screen shows the slide and lower part is reserved for presenter's notes. The scroll bar and buttons at the right edge of the screen can be used to move from one page to another.

ℹ️ *It is not <u>always</u> necessary to use this view to add notes. There is a **Notes** pane in **Normal** view that can be resized by dragging the border between the panes. If graphics are required however, they must be inserted in **Notes Page** view.*

⟲ Manoeuvres

1. Using the current presentation, display the **View** tab and select **Notes Page** in the **Presentation Views** group.

2. Use the scroll bar, if necessary, to move to the notes for slide **5**.

3. Click on the **Zoom** button on the **View** tab and choose **100%** from the dialog box, then click **OK**.

ℹ️ *Zoom percentage can also be controlled using a slider on the right of the **Status Bar**.*

4. The bottom half of the page should now be visible, with the words **Click to add text**. If this notes area is not visible, try scrolling the page up and down using the scroll bar.

5. Click on the words **Click to add text**. The words disappear and the box is highlighted. Type the following note:

   This is a notes page. Speaker's notes can be added here so that the presenter knows what to say when this slide is being shown.

6. Click on the white space outside the notes area to finish entering the text. Zoom to **50%** to see the whole page.

7. Switch to **Normal** view and move to slide **1**.

8. Click in the **Notes** pane and add the following note, zooming in if necessary:

   This is the first slide.

9. Switch to **Notes Page** view to confirm that the note is there.

Driving Lesson 16 - Slide Show

▣ Park and Read

Slide Show is used to view slides, one at a time, as an on screen presentation. This gives the creator an opportunity to view the presentation as others will see it. It is particularly useful in viewing the full effect of animations and transitions.

While the slide show is in progress, the mouse can be used to draw on the slide to highlight key points and notes can be added to individual slides.

☞ Manoeuvres

1. Using the presentation from the previous Driving Lesson, click the **Slide Show** button on the **View** tab. The slide show starts, with the first slide filling the screen.

2. Click the mouse button or press <**Page Down**> to move to the next slide.

3. To move back to the first slide, press <**Page Up**> or click the right mouse button and select **Previous** from the shortcut menu.

4. To move to a non-adjacent slide, click the right mouse button and select **Go to Slide** from the shortcut menu. Select **8 Visualise It** and that slide will be displayed.

ℹ *The shortcut menu can also be displayed by clicking the popup menu button,*

, that appears at the lower left corner of each slide.

5. Display the shortcut menu (using the method shown in the note above) and click the pointer button. This displays the **Pointer Menu**. Select **Ballpoint Pen** from the menu. The mouse pointer changes into a small dot.

6. Move the pen on to the slide and click and drag. The pointer draws a line on the slide. All lines drawn with any pen are saved to the presentation. Select **Erase All Ink on Slide** from the **Pointer Menu** to delete the lines drawn.

7. Display the **Pointer Menu** again this time select **Arrow** to return the mouse pointer to normal. View the rest of the presentation. When the end of the show is reached, a black screen appears, with the words **End of slide show, click to exit.**

ℹ *If this black screen does not appear, view **PowerPoint Options** and click the **Advanced** button. Select the **End with black slide** option, click **OK** and view the show again.*

8. Click once to return to the last view used.

Driving Lesson 17 - Saving a Presentation

Park and Read

A presentation must be saved if it is to be used again. There are two main ways to save: **Save** to save a new presentation or to update changes made to an existing one, **Save As** to save a presentation under a new name, or to a different location or in a different format.

Manoeuvres

1. The presentation opened earlier is now going to be saved. Click the **Office Button** and select **Save** (the **Save** button, ▣, or the key press **<Ctrl S>** can also be used).

2. From the dialog box, choose **Documents** from the **Favorite Links Bar** (if not already there by default).

3. Double click on **CIA DATA FILES** then **ECDL**, then on **6 Presentations**.

4. In the **File name** box, type **PowerPoint 2007**, replacing any existing text.

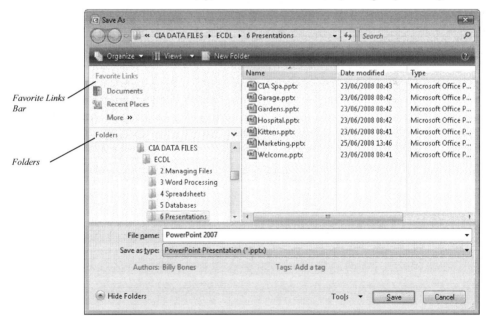

Driving Lesson 17 - Continued

5. Click on the drop down arrow at the right of the **Save as type** box to see the different formats available, including: text format **Outline/RTF** (*.rtf), **PowerPoint Template** (*.potx), earlier versions of *PowerPoint*, e.g. **PowerPoint 97-2003** (*.ppt), graphics formats including **JPEG File** (*.jpg) and **Windows Metafile** (*wmf).

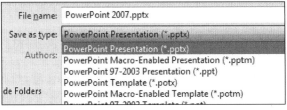

6. Choose the default format **PowerPoint Presentation (*.pptx)**.

7. Click the **Save** button, **Save** .

8. To save the presentation in a different format, or another name, select **Office Button** and then **Save As**.

9. The presentation is to be saved as an **Outline** file. This means that a presentation saved as an **rtf (Rich Text Format)** outline can be opened in various programs such as *Word*, although any graphic content will be lost.

10. Change the **File name** to **My Outline** and from **Save as type** select **Outline/RTF(*.rtf)**, then click **Save**.

11. To make sure that the file has been saved correctly, click the **Office Button** and select **Open**, ensure the location where your files are saved is selected and change to **All Files (*.*)**, to the right of the **File name** box.

12. The **Outline** file should appear as ![My Outline.rtf] . This icon indicates that only the text has been saved.

13. Click the **Cancel** button to close the **Open** dialog box.

14. A presentation can be saved in a special format - a **PowerPoint Show** - that allows people who don't have PowerPoint installed to view it. Click the **Office Button** and select **Save As**, then **PowerPoint Show**. Change the **File name** to **My Show**(*.ppsx) and click **Save**.

15. Repeat step 12 and notice the icon, ![My Show.ppsx]. Close the dialog box.

 Remember that files can be saved to any folder or to a particular folder that you have been instructed to use.

 *To be able to post a presentation to the World Wide Web, select **Save As** and select **Web Page** to save the presentation in the correct format.*

Driving Lesson 18 - Closing a Presentation

▣ Park and Read

To clear the screen and begin working on a new presentation, the current one can be closed. If the presentation has not been previously saved, or if it has been modified in any way, a prompt to save it will appear.

⌐ Manoeuvres

1.   With the presentation from the previous Driving Lesson on screen, click the **Office Button** and select **Close**. If no changes to the presentation have been made since it was saved in the previous Driving Lesson the presentation will close immediately.

2.   If any further changes have been made to the presentation, there will be a message asking if the new version of the presentation is to be saved, e.g. **Do you want to save the changes you made to PowerPoint 2007.pptx?** Click on **No**. The presentation now closes without saving.

ℹ️   *At the prompt box, clicking* **Yes** *would start the* **Save** *process. Clicking* **No** *would close the presentation without saving anything. Clicking* **Cancel** *will cancel the close process and return to the presentation.*

3.   A blank *PowerPoint* screen is now shown, ready to start a new presentation, open an existing one or close *PowerPoint*.

Driving Lesson 19 - Opening Presentations

▣ Park and Read

Once created and saved, a presentation can be opened at any time.

⌇ Manoeuvres

1. Click the **Office Button** and select 📂 _Open_ to display the **Open** dialog box.

ℹ️ *Alternatively, use the key press <**Ctrl O**>.*

2. Check that the location of the files is the **6 Presentations** folder, if not, click on **Documents** from the **Favorite Links** bar to view the contents of that folder, then double click on **CIA DATA FILES**, then **ECDL** and finally on **6 Presentations**.

3. The **PowerPoint 2007** presentation should be listed. Click on it once to select it, then click ⬚ _Open_ ▾ to open the presentation.

4. Move to the **Notes** page for slide **5**. Use zoom if necessary to see the text. Change **This is a notes page** to **This is an interesting notes page**.

5. The presentation has been changed, but a copy of the original is required, so use **Save As** to save the presentation as **PPT2** and leave it open.

6. Now open the two presentations called **Hospital** and **Gardens**, which should also be in this folder, using the **Open** button.

7. Practise switching between the presentations by clicking on their button in the **Taskbar**, then close all the presentations <u>without</u> saving.

Driving Lesson 20 - New Presentations

▣ Park and Read

When creating a new presentation with a **Blank Presentation** template, all that has to be specified is the type of slide to be used, i.e. Title slide, Title and Content, etc. A blank slide will be produced, without colours, background, graphics, etc.

𝕽 Manoeuvres

1.　Click the **Office Button** and then **New** to display the **New Presentation** dialog box.

2.　Click on **Blank Presentation** under **Blank and recent**. Click **Create** to start a new, blank presentation.

3.　The **Layout** button is on the **Slides** group, **Home** tab. The default layout **Title Slide** should be selected by default, Click on the **Layout** button, and then on a few other layouts to see how the view in the **Slide** pane changes. Finally, click on the **Title Slide** layout again.

4.　A completely blank presentation slide has been created. Text can be added to the boxes as indicated.

5.　Switch to each of the different views in turn to see the effect. From this position, any aspect of the presentation can be defined.

6.　**Close** the presentation <u>without</u> saving.

ⓘ *Usually, all presentations start with a **Title Slide** to introduce the presentation.*

Driving Lesson 21 - Creating a Presentation

Park and Read

A variety of ways to create and view a presentation have now been examined. From this point onwards, a presentation will be created using the major features of *PowerPoint*.

Themes provide a common style throughout a presentation. This includes a common background, and related colours for text and graphics

Manoeuvres

1. Click the **Office Button** and select **New**. At the **New Presentation** dialog box, click on **Installed Themes**.

2. From the list of themes, select a few to see how they appear in the preview at the right of the dialog box. Finally select the theme **Flow** and click **Create**.

> *Many more slide themes are available from **Microsoft Office Online**. Select **Design Slides** from the **New Presentation** dialog box.*

3. The first (**Title**) slide in the presentation has now been created with the **Flow** design applied. Notice how the **Status Bar** shows **Slide 1 of 1**.

4. Make sure **Normal** view is selected.

5. On the **Title Slide** of the new presentation, click on the area **Click to add title** and type the title **CIA Training Ltd**.

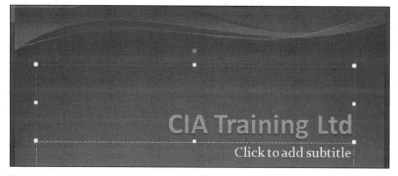

6. Click on the **Click to add subtitle** area and type **A PowerPoint Presentation**.

> *If it is not possible to complete the remainder of the guide in one session, then save the presentation, at any time, as **CIA**, and continue at a later date.*

Driving Lesson 22 - Adding and Deleting Slides

▣ Park and Read

A new slide can be added to the presentation at any time and at any place. New slides are placed directly after the slide that is currently selected. If necessary, their position can easily be changed later using the **Slides** pane or **Slide Sorter** view.

Make sure that each slide has a different title. This makes it much easier to navigate between slides in **Slide Show View**, or to distinguish between slides in **Outline View** or other views. It's also good practice to be concise when entering text on slides, e.g. use short phrases and bullet points or numbered lists instead of long sentences. The idea of a presentation is that you expand on these brief points when delivering it.

Manoeuvres

1. From the **Home** tab, click the drop down arrow on the **New Slide** button.

2. A panel of available layouts is displayed. **Title Slide** and the **Title Only** slide formats are often used to start presentations. Other formats are used to display content. Click on the layout, **Title Only**.

3. The new slide, number **2**, has now been created. The **Status Bar** now shows **Slide 2 of 2**.

4. Use the **New Slide** button to create a third slide, this time with the **Two Content** layout. The **Status Bar** now shows **Slide 3 of 3**.

[i] *To position a new slide in a particular place, click between the required slides in* **Slides** *view or* **Slide Sorter** *view and then insert the new slide.*

5. On slide **3**, click to add the title **Presentation Agenda**. Notice the handles around the text. These can be used to resize the text area.

6. Click at the top of the first column of text and type **The Company**. Press <Enter> and type **The People**, then on the next line, type **The Products**.

    > Presentation Agenda
    > • The Company   • Sales
    > • The People   • Drawing
    > • The Products   • Advert

7. In the second column of text, enter **Sales** on the first line, **Drawing** on the second and **Advert** on the third line.

8. Select slide **2** by clicking on it in the **Slides Pane**, then click **Delete**, ✖ Delete or press the <**Delete**> key. The slide is removed.

9. **Save** the presentation as **CIA** to the data file location and leave it open.

Driving Lesson 23 - Changing Slide Layout

▣ Park and Read

The layout of a slide can be changed after it has been added to a presentation.

⌖ Manoeuvres

1. On slide **2 Presentation Agenda**, click and drag the mouse over the text in the left column to highlight it and then press <**Delete**>.

2. Repeat this for the text in the right column.

3. To change the type of slide, on the **Home** tab, click 🔲 Layout ▾ from the **Slides** group.

4. From the drop down menu, select the **Title and Content** layout.

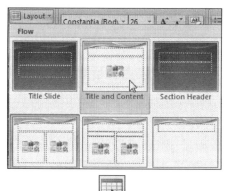

5. On the slide, click the table icon, 🔲 to display the **Insert Table** dialog box.

6. Change the value in the **Number of columns** box to **2** and the **Number of rows** box to **3**.

7. Click **OK** to create the table, then with the cursor in the first cell type **The Company**.

8. On second thoughts, a bulleted list would be more appropriate. Click exactly on the table border to select the whole table (the pointer becomes a four headed arrow) and press <**Delete**> to remove the table.

9. Click the **Layout** button again and select the **Two Content** layout.

10. Retype the original text - the picture on the previous page should help.

11. Save the presentation and leave it open.

Driving Lesson 24 - Background Colour

Park and Read

The background colour of specific slides or all slides can be changed. However, it is preferable not to use too many different colours in the same presentation.

Manoeuvres

1. In **Normal** view, add two new slides, both **Two Content** layout, after slide **2**.

2. Switch to **Slide Sorter** view and select slide **3**.

3. Select the **Design** tab from the **Ribbon** and click the **Background** dialog box launcher.

4. Select **Fill** from the list on the left. From the list at the right of the box, select the **Solid fill** option.

5. Click the **Color** button, 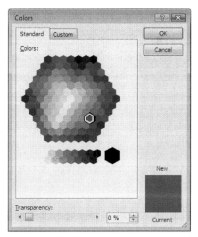 and then **More Colors**. Select the **Standard** tab from the **Colors** dialog box. Select a vivid **pink** from the honeycomb.

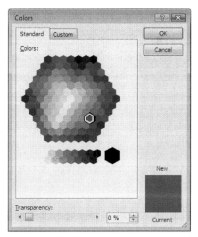

6. Click **OK**. To apply the new background to slide **3** only click **Close** (**Apply to All** would change the colour of all slides).

7. In the same way, select slide **4** and change its background colour to yellow.

8. Delete slide **4** by making sure it is selected and then pressing <**Delete**>.

9. Delete slide **3** and close the presentation, saving the changes.

Driving Lesson 25 - Revision

This covers the features introduced in this section. Try not to refer to the preceding Driving Lessons while completing it.

1.   Create a **New Blank Presentation** selecting the **Title Slide** layout.

2.   Click on the title slide and add title text **Put Your IT Skills to the Test**.

3.   Click to add the Subtitle **'by *Your Name'*.**

4.   Insert a **New Slide** using the **Title and Text** layout.

5.   Click to add the title **Introduction**.

6.   Click to add the following bullet points:

- **Concepts of ICT**
- **Using the computer and managing files**
- **Word processing**
- **Spreadsheets**
- **Using databases**
- **Presentation**
- **Web browsing and communication**

7.   Save the file naming it **IT Skills**.

8.   Close the presentation.

If you experienced any difficulty completing the Revision, refer back to the Driving Lessons in this section. Then redo the Revision.

Driving Lesson 26 - Revision

This covers the features introduced in this section. Try not to refer to the preceding Driving Lessons while completing it.

1.   Open the presentation **CIA Spa**.

2.   View the notes page for the first slide.

3.   Use the **Zoom** control to change the magnification of the page to **100%**.

4.   Insert the following text into the notes page area.

> **Good morning ladies and gentlemen, welcome to CiA Lodge.**
>
> **I am (your name) and I will be your speaker for this presentation.**
>
> **First of all I would like to give you a brief introduction to the business.**

5.   Use the **zoom** control to display the whole page.

6.   Change to **Slide Sorter** view and select slide **2**.

7.   Display the slide in **Notes Page** view and insert the following text:

> **Since 1985 CiA Lodge has been a successful hotel and spa.**
>
> **Every treatment is uniquely customised to our guests' requirements. Our aim is to ensure that each guest receives the benefit of personal attention. Our philosophy has resulted in many repeat bookings and a regular clientele.**

8.   Make sure the option is set to end the presentation with a black end slide. Switch to **Slide Show** view.

9.   View the whole show.

10.   Save the presentation as **CIA Lodge**.

11.   Close the presentation.

If you experienced any difficulty completing the Revision, refer back to the Driving Lessons in this section. Then redo the Revision.

Once you are confident with the features, complete the Record of Achievement Matrix referring to the section at the end of the guide. Only when competent move on to the next Section.

Section 3
Formatting

By the end of this Section you should be able to:

Apply Formatting, Text Effects and Bullets

Use Undo and Redo

Change Alignment and Spacing

Use Cut, Copy and Paste

Use Animation Schemes and Custom Animation

Apply Headers & Footers

Work with Slide Master

Check Spelling

To gain an understanding of the above features, work through the **Driving Lessons** in this **Section**.

For each **Driving Lesson**, read the **Park and Read** instructions, without touching the keyboard, then work through the numbered steps of the **Manoeuvres** on the computer. Complete the **Revision Exercise(s)** at the end of the section to test your knowledge.

Driving Lesson 27 - Formatting: Font & Size

▣ Park and Read

The text on any slide can be formatted in a number of ways, including changing the font, size, appearance, colour, alignment, etc. Many of the normal features of word processing are available when entering or editing text on a slide.

⌐ Manoeuvres

1. Open the **CIA** presentation and view the **Presentation Agenda** slide in **Normal** view.

2. Click and drag the mouse over the text in the first column to select it.

3. From the **Home** tab, click on the **Font** drop down arrow, | Constantia (Bod) ▾ | and choose a different font from the list, e.g. **Tahoma**.

4. Using the **Font Size** list, | 26 ▾ |, choose a larger size of font.

5. Click on the **Increase Font Size** button, | A |.

6. If necessary, change the font size so that each item in the column is at its maximum size but still fits on one line.

7. With the text still highlighted, click the **Font** dialog box launcher to display the dialog box (the **Font** dialog box will probably have different selections made).

8. Choose the **Arial Black** font and enter size **28** from the dialog box. Click **OK**.

9. Leave the presentation open.

Driving Lesson 28 - Undo and Redo

Park and Read

The **Undo** and **Redo** functions can be really useful, for example if something is deleted by mistake the deletion can be undone. **Undo** cancels the last action performed and **Redo** cancels the **Undo** action, leaving the presentation as it was originally.

Manoeuvres

1. Viewing the **Presentation Agenda** slide in the **CIA** presentation, select the text in the second column.

2. Press <**Delete**>.

3. Hold the mouse over the **Undo** button to see the **ToolTip**.

4. To replace the deleted text, click the button.

*The wording after **Undo** and **Redo** changes depending on the action last performed.*

5. To delete the text again, click **Redo Clear**, .

6. Click **Undo**, , to replace the text.

7. Click the drop down arrow at the right of the **Undo** button, to see all of the actions that could be reversed.

> Character Style
> Increase Font Size
> Font Size
> Replace Fonts
> Delete Slide

8. Click **Redo clear**, , to remove the text again.

9. **Undo** the deletion.

10. Leave the presentation open.

Driving Lesson 29 - Applying Text Effects

▣ Park and Read

Various effects such as bold, italic, underline and shadow can be applied to selected text on a presentation slide. Text colour can also be changed.

ℝ Manoeuvres

1. Using the **Presentation Agenda** slide in the **CIA** presentation,, select the text in the second column.

2. Click the **Bold** button, [B], to see the effect on the text. Try the **Italic**, [I], and **Underline**, [U], in turn. Apply a shadow by clicking **Text Shadow**, [S].

3. Remove all the effects from the second column and apply the shadow effect to the first column.

4. Text can be offset from its normal position using subscript and superscript. Add a new **Title and Content** slide and add the title **Text Effects**.

5. For the first bullet, type **CIATM** and for the second bullet type **H2O**. Select the letters **TM** from the first bullet, then click the **Font** dialog box launcher and check the **Superscript** box then click **OK**.

    • CIA^{TM}
    • H_2O

6. Notice how a "trademark" symbol has been created. Now select the **2** from the second bullet and display the **Font** dialog box again, this time selecting **Subscript** before clicking **OK**.

7. Select all of the text, excluding the title. Click the drop down arrow on the **Font Colour** button, [A ▾]. The colour box appears.

8. The colours already used or pre-defined as appropriate to this background are shown (**Theme Colors**). Select any available colour or click **More Colors** to choose a new colour from the honeycomb, then click **OK**.

9. With the text still selected, display the **Font** dialog box. Select any effects and colours desired. Click **OK** to see the effect. Note that some effects cannot be seen properly while the text is still selected.

ℹ️ *Text cannot be both* ***Superscript*** *and* ***Subscript***.

10. Delete this slide from the presentation by switching to **Slide Sorter** view, ensuring the **Text Effects** slide is selected and pressing <**Delete**>.

Driving Lesson 30 - Alignment, Spacing & Case

▣ Park and Read

Alignment of the text, spacing and case can be altered to suit the user. Spacing out the text can sometimes make it easier to read.

↻ Manoeuvres

1. Using the **Presentation Agenda** slide in **Normal** view, select all the text in the first column.

2. From the **Home** tab, click the **Center** button, ▤, from the **Paragraph** group and then the **Align Text Left** button, ▤, to see the difference.

3. Click **Align Text Right**, ▤. Revert back to **Left** aligned.

4. Text can also be aligned vertically in a text box. Click on the left text box and click the **Align Text** button, ▤, from the **Paragraph** group.

5. Select **Bottom** to anchor the text to the bottom of the box. Click the **Undo** button to revert the alignment to the **Top** (the default).

6. Select the text in the first column. Click the **Line Spacing** button, ▤▾, and click **2.0** to double space the text.

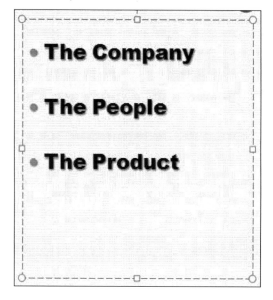

Driving Lesson 30 - Continued

7. Use the button to change the line spacing back to **1**.

8. Click the **Line Spacing** button and select **Line Spacing Options**.

9. Change the spacing both **Before** and **After** to **24 pt** by typing in the appropriate boxes.

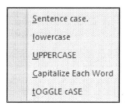

10. Click **OK** and notice the difference in how the text is spaced compared to the other column.

11. With the text in the second column selected, click **Change Case** button, **Aa** from the **Font** group.

| Sentence case. |
| lowercase |
| UPPERCASE |
| Capitalize Each Word |
| tOGGLE cASE |

12. Select **UPPERCASE**. The text will now be all in upper case.

13. Click the same button and select **lowercase**.

14. Now choose to **Capitalize Each Word**. The text is back to its original format.

15. Practise changing the alignment and spacing.

16. Change the text in both columns back to normal (left aligned, single line spacing, **6.72** pt before paragraph and **0** pt after paragraph).

Driving Lesson 31 - Bullets

▣ Park and Read

Text in a list is usually **bulleted**; the type, colour and size of the bullet can be changed. Bullets can also be selected from a grid containing all the symbol characters associated with different fonts.

⌐ Manoeuvres

1. With the text in the first column of the **Presentation Agenda** slide selected, click the **Bullets** button, ▤, to remove the bullets. Click the button again to reapply them.

2. Bulleted text can also have an indent applied to move it further to the right. Select the text in the first column and click **Increase List Level**, ▤.

3. With it still selected, click **Decrease List Level**, ▤, removing the indent.

4. Click the drop down arrow on the **Bullets** button, select a different bullet.

5. Drop down the options again and select **Bullets and Numbering**. The **Bullets and Numbering** dialog box appears.

6. Choose a different bullet from the options, select a different colour and size, then click **OK**

7. Display the dialog box again and practise changing bullet types, by clicking the **Customize** button and selecting various characters from the grid. Different fonts can be displayed using the **Font** drop down list - select any **Wingdings** to show the variety of picture options for bullets.

8. With the first column selected, display the **Bullets and Numbering** dialog box and select the **Numbered** tab.

9. To number the text, select any **1,2,3** option (an example is shown opposite) and click **OK**.

10. Change the numbering to lower case Roman numerals, i.e. **i,ii,iii**.

11. Now reapply any bullet style to the first column of bullets.

12. Once the bullets in the first column have been changed, apply the same bullet style and text formatting to the second column and leave the presentation open.

Driving Lesson 32 - Cut & Paste

 Park and Read

The **Cut** and **Paste** commands allow text and other items, such as graphics or slides to be moved around a presentation from one place to another, quickly and easily. When an item is cut, it is removed from its original location.

When copied or cut, text is placed in a temporary storage area known as the **Clipboard**. Up to **24** cut or copied items can be held on the **Clipboard**, which is common to all *Windows* applications.

Manoeuvres

1. Click the **Clipboard** launcher to display the **Office Clipboard Task Pane**. If it contains any items, click ⌧ Clear All to delete them.

2. Position the cursor in the first line of text on the **Presentation Agenda** slide - **The Company**. Select the word **The**, press the <**Delete**> key to delete the word and then type in **Our**. Add a space if necessary.

3. Select the first line of text, **Our Company**. Make sure the selection includes the space after the text.

4. Click on the **Cut** button, ✂, from the **Clipboard** group and the text is removed from the slide and placed on the **Clipboard**, where it is represented by an icon.

 Alternatively use the key press <***Ctrl X***> *to cut items and place them in the* ***Clipboard***.

5. Place the cursor at the end of **The Products** and press <**Enter**> to create a new bullet and empty line. Click on the icon from the **Clipboard** to paste the text at the new location.

 Text can be moved to a different slide in the same way.

Driving Lesson 32 - Continued

6.   A **Smart Tag** called **Paste Options** will be displayed, 🗐. This controls whether the pasted text keeps the formatting it had originally or takes on the formatting of the destination. It is only relevant if the text being pasted has a different format to its target location. Click the **Smart Tag** to see the options then click on a blank area of the slide to remove them.

ℹ️   *Bullets can pose problems when cutting and pasting. Sometimes blank bullet lines are left behind or created during the process. Press <**Backspace**> when on an empty line to remove the line and the bullet.*

7.   Click and drag to select the line **The People** and cut it, using any method.

8.   Open the **PPT2** presentation in **Normal** view and move to slide **3, Superior Text**.

9.   Place the cursor at the end of the slide text and press <**Enter**> to create a new line.

10. Instead of using the **Clipboard** display, the **Paste** button or the key press <**Ctrl V**> can always be used to paste the last item cut or copied.

11. Click the **Paste** button to paste the text **The People** from the **CIA** presentation.

12. Click the **Smart Tag** to see the paste options and select **Keep Text Only** to ensure that the pasted text takes on the formatting of existing text.

13. Change to **Slide Sorter** view and click on the slide **2** to select it. Now click on the **Cut** button and the slide disappears.

14. To reposition the removed slide, place the cursor to the right of the slide **4** and click on the **Paste** button.

15. Slides can moved between presentations in the same way as text. Select slide **5** and click the **Cut** button.

16. Use the **Taskbar** to display the **CiA** presentation and select the last slide.

17. Click on the **Paste** button. The slide from **PPT2** is inserted.

ℹ️   *The setting **Use Destination Theme** in the **Paste Options Smart Tag** will ensure that the pasted slide takes on the default formatting of the target presentation.*

18. Leave both presentations open.

Driving Lesson 33 - Copy & Paste

 Park and Read

Text, graphics and slides may also be copied. When this action is carried out, the item stays in its original place and a copy of it is placed on the **Clipboard**.

An item that has been cut or copied may be pasted any number of times.

Items can be copied within a slide, between slides, or between presentations.

Manoeuvres

1. In **Normal** view, select **Our Company** on the **Presentation Agenda** slide of the **CiA** presentation. Click on the **Copy** button, ⬛.

 Alternatively use the key press <Ctrl C> to copy items.

2. Look at the **Clipboard** to see that a copy of **Our Company** has been placed there, while the original text has stayed in place.

3. Place the insertion point just after the **s** of **The Products** and press <**Enter**> to create a new bullet and empty line for the copied text to be pasted into. Click on the most recent **Our Company** icon from the **Clipboard** to paste the copied text into the slide at the new location.

 *The **Paste** button, on the Ribbon, or the key press <Ctrl V> can be used to paste the last item cut or copied.*

4. If a new line is not started automatically, press <**Enter**> again to start one and click the **Paste** button. The copied text is pasted again.

 *The **Paste Smart Tag**, can appear and be used in exactly the same way as with cutting and pasting.*

5. Delete the last two insertions of **Our Company**.

6. Use <**Backspace**> to remove all unnecessary blank bullet lines from the list. Remove any extra space.

7. Close the **Clipboard**.

8. Change to **Slide Sorter** view and click on the slide, slide **2**, **Presentation Agenda**.

9. Now click on the **Copy** button, ⬛.

Driving Lesson 33 - Continued

10. To paste a copy of the slide, place the cursor on the last slide (slide **3**) and click on the **Paste** button. A copy of the **Presentation Agenda** is added to the end of the presentation.

11. Use the **Taskbar** to move to the **PPT2** presentation.

12. In **Slide Sorter** view, place the cursor between slides **2** and **3**.

13. Click . This pastes the last object copied, the **Presentation Agenda** slide, into the **PPT2** presentation. Notice that the current slide theme is automatically applied to it, but this could be changed by using the **Paste Options Smart Tag**.

14. In the **PPT2** presentation, delete the pasted slide, number **3**.

15. Text can be copied between presentations in the same way. On slide **2**, select the **Title** text **Superior Text** and click on the **Copy** button, ▣.

16. Use the **Taskbar** to move to the **CiA** presentation.

17. Display slide **4** and select the title text. Click the **Paste** button. The text **Superior Text** is pasted in and replaces the original text.

18. In the **CIA** presentation, delete slides **3** and **4**.

19. Close the **PPT2** presentation <u>without</u> saving.

20. Leave the **CiA** presentation open.

Driving Lesson 34 - Standard Animation

▣ Park and Read

Animation can be applied to text and objects on a slide so they appear on the slide in a variety of different ways, e.g. fly from top, dissolve, etc. Custom animation can be applied in 3 possible areas: **Slide Transition** (how the slide comes into the presentation), **Title Animation** (how the title appears on the screen) and **Body Animation** (how the rest of the slide appears). Standard animation can quickly be applied to specific areas of a slide.

↷ Manoeuvres

1. Show slide **1**, **CIA Training Ltd** in **Normal** view. Select the title text.

2. From the **Animations** tab, click the drop down arrow on **Animate**,

    > 📇 Animate: | No Animation ▾ |

    .

ℹ *To remove animation, select **No Animation** from this list.*

3. Move the mouse over **Fade** and the effect is shown on the slide.

4. Click **Wipe** to apply this animation.

5. Click 🖳 on the **Status Bar** to see how the slide will actually appear. The slide appears immediately. Click with the mouse to trigger the title text. Press <**Esc**> to return to **Normal** view.

6. Now select the subtitle and apply **Fly In - All At Once** from the **Animation** list.

ℹ *Animation properties such as triggers, timings and sound can only be applied by using the **Custom Animation** feature.*

7. Click **Preview**, | Preview | on the **Ribbon** to see the slide animation.

ℹ *In **Slide Sorter** view and the **Slides** pane, slides with animation are indicated by a star symbol.*

8. View the **Slide Show** to see how the presentation is affected. Remember to click with the mouse where necessary to trigger the next text item.

9. Press <**Esc**> to end the show and return to **Normal** view. Leave the presentation open for the next Driving Lesson.

Driving Lesson 35 - Custom Animation

▣ Park and Read

Custom animation allows effects for individual items to be chosen from 4 areas:

> **Entrance** effects (how an item comes onto the screen),
>
> **Emphasis** effects (what it does on the screen),
>
> **Exit** effects (how an item disappears)
>
> **Motion Paths** (to move an item around a slide).

More than one animation effect can be applied to the same item.

Customising also allows greater control over such details as the timing and order of the animations, sounds, and the appearance of text after animation. For any selected effect, all the options can be set from a dialog box with 3 tabs.

The **Effect** tab controls the addition of sounds, what happens to the item after animation and whether text appears all at once, word by word or letter by letter.

The **Timing** tab controls when an effect is activated - on the click of the mouse or automatically, how fast the effect runs and whether it repeats.

The **Text Animation** tab controls how the effects are applied to a bulleted text list (either to the whole list or by heading/subheading).

Manoeuvres

1. In **Normal** view make sure the first (**Title**) slide is selected. From the **Animations** tab, click **Custom Animation**, 〖🔟 Custom Animation〗. The **Custom Animation Task Pane** will be displayed.

2. The individual animated objects set up by the **Animation Scheme** for this slide are listed in the **Task Pane**. Click on the **Title 1** area of the slide in the **Slide** pane at the right of **Normal** view.

3. Notice the text areas on the slide have numbered boxes showing the sequence in which they will be animated. The sequence is also shown in the list of animation effects in the **Custom Animation Task Pane**.

   | 1 🎯 | ✶ Title 1: CIA Trainin... ▾ |
   | 2 🎯 | ✶ A PowerPoint Presenta... |

4. Click on the **Re-Order** down arrow to animate the **Title** after the text. Click the up arrow to return the **Title** to the top of the order again.

☞

Driving Lesson 35 - Continued

5. The **Title 1** line in the effects list is already selected, click the **Change** button at the top of the pane and select **Entrance** to see a list of alternative entrance effects. Try out some of the effects and then select **Spiral In** (select **More Effects** and scroll to the **Exciting** group). Click **OK**.

6. Click the drop down arrow on the **Title 1:** line.

7. Select **Effect Options** to display the dialog box to set all animation controls for the selected effect. Make sure the **Effect** tab is selected.

8. Click in the **Sound** box to display the sounds available to accompany the animation. Select a sound if required.

9. Click in the **Animate text** box, and select to introduce the text **By word**.

10. Select the **Timing** tab and look at the options available. Change the **Speed** setting for the **Medium** effect.

11. Click **OK** in the dialog box to preview the effect that has just been amended.

12. Click the **Play** button in the **Custom Animation Task Pane** to preview all the current animation.

13. Experiment with different effects and settings and then close the **Custom Animation Task Pane**.

14. Save and close the **CIA** presentation.

Driving Lesson 36 - Spell Checking

 Park and Read

A presentation can be checked at any time for spelling errors, including repeated words. The spell checker is the same as that in *Word*, it will suggest alternatives for words it does not recognise; these can be accepted or ignored or in the case of a repeated word, deleted. Words can be added to the dictionary if desired.

Right clicking on an incorrectly spelled word displays a shortcut menu listing possible alternatives.

Manoeuvres

1. Open the **Marketing** presentation (words spelled incorrectly will be underlined with a red wavy line).

2. Select the **Review** tab from the **Ribbon**.

3. Click on the **Spelling** button, to start the spell checker. The spelling for the whole presentation will be checked.

4. When the **Spelling** dialog box appears, either click **Ignore** to leave the selected word unchanged or click **Change** to replace the word. The word can be replaced by selecting one from the **Suggestions** list or by typing a new word into the **Change to** box.

*If necessary, the dialog box can be moved to see the context of the word before making a selection from **Suggestions**. Just click and drag on its blue **Title Bar**.*

Spelling		? ✕
Not in Dictionary:	lndscape	
Change to:	landscape	Ignore / Ignore All
Suggestions:	landscape	Change / Change All
		Add / Suggest
Options...		AutoCorrect / Close

5. A repeated word will be reported as a possible mistake, and a **Delete** button will be made available. Click this to remove the duplicate word.

6. When finished spell checking, click **OK** (if any mistakes were corrected or repeated words deleted). Close the **Spelling** dialog box, if necessary.

7. Leave the presentation on screen for the next Driving Lesson.

Driving Lesson 37 - Master Pages

Park and Read

Master pages contain text or graphics that are to be displayed on every page of a presentation. There are different master pages for: **Slides**, **Handouts** and **Notes**, which act as templates, to allow consistent formatting, text and graphics to be applied to the slides, notes and handouts accompanying the presentation.

Manoeuvres

1. Using the **Marketing** presentation, click on slide **1**. Select the **View** tab and click **Slide Master**. Select the main **Slide Master** (the top thumbnail) to display it in the main **Slide** pane. Anything put on this slide will appear on every slide.

*In the left pane, the default design **Slide Master** is shown at the top. Beneath that is the master for the **Title Slide** layout (used by slide **1**). The remaining slides show all the masters for all other available layouts.*

2. Click the **Insert** tab and select **Text Box**. Click and drag the mouse to create a text box on the right side of the master slide.

3. Type **This text may appear on every slide**

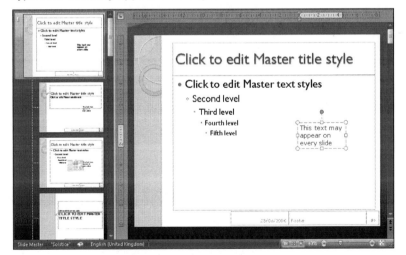

4. Select **Normal** view. The text entered on to the master slide appears on every slide. It may be obscured by other material on the slide - it is better to create the master slide before adding material to the individual slides.

Driving Lesson 37 - Continued

5. Go into **Slide Master** view again, ensure the **Slide Master** is selected from the left pane and click on **Click to edit Master title style**. Format the title so that it is centre aligned and underlined.

6. Return to **Normal** view - all the slides titles now have this formatting.

7. Return to the **Slide Master** and remove the text box entered earlier by clicking on the text to display the text box. Click on the edge of the text box and press <**Delete**>.

8. To insert an imported object (a picture called **Photo** from the data files supplied with this module) on the master slide, display the **Insert** tab and click on **Picture**.

9. Ensure that the location of the supplied data files is displayed at the top of the **Insert Picture** dialog box. Select the picture **Photo** and then click **Insert**.

10. Resize the photo by clicking on one of the corners, (the cursor should change to ⬉), and dragging inwards, until it is about half its original size.

11. Move it to the bottom right corner by clicking in the centre, (the cursor should change to ✛), and dragging.

ℹ️ *Working with objects in PowerPoint will be covered in more detail in the next Section.*

12. In **Normal** view, notice that the photo appears on every slide in the presentation.

13. To remove the photo, return to the **Slide Master** slide, click on the photo to select it and press <**Delete**>.

14. To change the background colour of all slides, click the **Background** dialog box launcher and select **Solid fill**.

15. Click **Color** and select a green square.

16. Click **Close** and switch to **Normal** view. As the change was applied to the **Slide Master**, all slide backgrounds have changed.

ℹ️ *In **Normal View**, this process would only change the background of the selected slide. It would be necessary to select **Apply to All**.*

ℹ️ *Note that with this **Theme**, the background makes up only a small part of a slide design. Some **Themes** can also define their own Slide Masters so that, objects on the main Slide Master may not appear on every other slide layout.*

17. Close the presentation <u>without</u> saving.

Driving Lesson 38 - Headers & Footers

P **Park and Read**

Headers and **Footers** are items of information that appear at the top and/or bottom of every slide, or notes and handouts. This information usually consists of the date, the page or slide number and text such as the company name. The date can be fixed or inserted as a field in a number of different formats.

Manoeuvres

1. Open the **CIA** presentation.

2. To apply a header and footer to slide **1** only, select it in **Normal** view, select the **Insert** tab and click **Header & Footer**.

3. Click on the **Slide** tab if not already selected.

4. Place a tick in the **Date and time** checkbox and select to update it automatically.

5. Click on the drop down arrow next to the box displaying the date and choose one of the available formats. The date will always be updated and always in this format.

6. Tick the **Slide number** checkbox so that the slide will be numbered.

7. Tick the **Footer** checkbox and in the text box type **CIA Training Ltd**.

8. Click **Apply** to apply only to the selected slide.

9. Look at slide **2** - there are no footers. Select slide **1** and select **Header & Footer** again.

10. To stop the date updating automatically select the **Fixed** option from **Date and time** and enter a specific date in the adjacent box. This date will always be shown. Click on **Apply to All** this time to apply the information to all of the slides.

11. View the **Header and Footer**, switch to the **Notes and Handouts** tab and select to have **Page numbers** and a **Footer** of **Compliments of CIA Training**. Click on **Apply to All** to apply this to all the notes / handouts.

12. View the slides in **Slide Sorter** view, then in **Notes Page** view to observe the different footers in each view.

13. Save the presentation and close it.

Driving Lesson 39 - Revision

This covers the features introduced in this section. Try not to refer to the preceding Driving Lessons while completing it.

1. Open the presentation **Welcome**.

2. Use the main **Slide Master** to apply the following formatting to all slides:

    Format all of the slide title fonts to **Tahoma**.

    Increase all the title text size to **48 pt**.

    Change the first level bulleted text (Master text style) for each of the slides to **24pt** and make them bold.

    Use the line spacing option format the bulleted lists on all slides to have **1.5 line spacing**.

    Insert a text box in the lower right corner with the text **Certified Organic**.

3. Select slide **2**, format the bullets using an arrow character of your choice.

4. Using slide **3** change the bullets to numbers.

5. Use the **Undo** command to undo the last action.

6. Use the **Redo** command to restore the numbers.

7. On slide **2** select the bullet **Founded in 1985...** and cut it from the list.

8. Paste the text at the bottom of the list as a new bulleted line. Delete any blank bulleted lines that may remain.

9. Create a new **Title and Content** slide at the end of the presentation with a title of **History**.

10. With the **Clipboard** task pane open, copy both the text **Founded in 1985...** from slide **2** and the third bullet from slide **3**.

11. Paste the last 2 copied items to make 2 bullet points on the **History** slide.

12. Ensure the same bullets are applied to both lines.

13. Run the slide show from slide **1**.

14. Save the presentation as **Welcome2** and close it.

If you experienced any difficulty completing the Revision, refer back to the Driving Lessons in this section. Then redo the Revision.

Driving Lesson 40 - Revision

This covers the features introduced in this section. Try not to refer to the preceding Driving Lessons while completing it.

1. Open the presentation **Garage** in **Normal** view.

2. Add a **Animation** effect of **Fade** to the Title and the text below the title.

3. Select each car manufacturer's name in turn and apply an **Animation** effect of **Wipe**.

i *To select the manufacturers names, click on an actual character from the text, when the cursor changes to a four way arrow.*

4. Apply an **Animation** effect of **Fly In** to all other objects.

5. Run the slide show. Click the mouse to start each effect.

6. Remove the effects from each car manufacturer's name.

7. Save the presentation as **Open Day** and close it.

If you experienced any difficulty completing the Revision, refer back to the Driving Lessons in this section. Then redo the Revision.

Once you are confident with the features, complete the Record of Achievement Matrix referring to the section at the end of the guide. Only when competent move on to the next Section.

Section 4
PowerPoint Objects

By the end of this Section you should be able to:

Insert and Modify an Organisation Chart

Move, Resize and Copy Objects

Insert and Animate Images

Insert a Chart

Use Drawing Tools and Shapes on Slides

Select, Rotate and Flip Objects

Arrange and Distribute Objects

Change Object Colours

Import Images

To gain an understanding of the above features, work through the **Driving Lessons** in this **Section**.

For each **Driving Lesson**, read the **Park and Read** instructions, without touching the keyboard, then work through the numbered steps of the **Manoeuvres** on the computer. Complete **Revision Exercise(s)** at the end of the section to test your knowledge.

Driving Lesson 41 - Organisation Charts

🅿 Park and Read

Slides in a presentation can include various objects which, although easy to insert, result in an impressive show. In a company presentation, it is often a good idea to insert an organisation chart to show the company's structure.

☞ Manoeuvres

1. Open the presentation **CIA** and insert a new slide after slide **2**, using the **Title and Content** layout.

2. Click **Insert SmartArt Graphic**, [icon], on the slide to display the **Choose a SmartArt Graphic** dialog box. Look at the diagrams available. Select **Hierarchy** from the left, choose the **Organization Chart** and click **OK**.

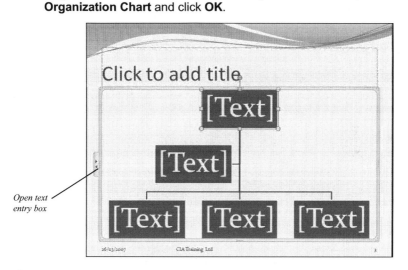

3. Add the slide title **Company Structure** and centre it.

4. Click on the organisation chart to select it, then click in the top box and type **Brian Brown**, press <**Enter**> and type **Director**.

5. Click in a blank part of the next box down to select it. Make sure the box is selected (the box outline will be a solid line) not the text content.

6. Press <**Delete**> to remove the box from the structure.

Driving Lesson 41 - Continued

7. Text can also be entered using the text entry box. Click the button on the left border of the chart to display it if it is not already shown.

8. Click on the next level down in the text entry box and type **Joanne Malone**. Hold down **<Shift>**, press **<Enter>** and type **Training Manager**.

9. Similarly, enter details for **Katherine Deacon, Supervisor** and **Jean Barker, Office Manager** into the next two bullet points.

10. Make sure the **SmartArt Tools Design** tab is shown on the **Ribbon** and select the shape for **Joanne Malone** on the chart.

11. Click the drop down arrow on **Add Shape**, from the **Create Graphic** group, and select **Add Shape Below**.

12. A subordinate box is created linked to Joanne's. Click in the new box and enter **Andrew Wilson, Trainer**.

13. Select the Joanne Malone shape, click the **Layout** button from the **Create Graphic** group, and select **Standard** to change the layout.

14. Select the Andrew Wilson shape and select **Add Shape After**. Another box is added at the same level (co-worker). Enter **Michael Jones, Trainer**.

15. Add **Susan Li, Clerk** as a subordinate (**Add Shape Below**) to Jean Barker.

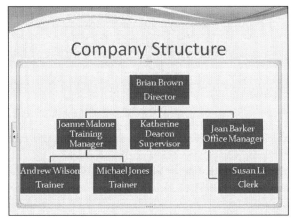

16. Look at the text entry box to see how the structure is represented there, then use the ☒ button to it. Leave the presentation open for the next Driving Lesson.

Driving Lesson 42 - Modify Organisation Chart

▣ Park and Read

It may be necessary to delete, move or resize an object after placing it on a slide. All objects can be resized or repositioned so that they occupy the correct amount of space and position.

Manoeuvres

1. With slide **3** in **Normal** view, make sure the organisation chart is selected by clicking on it once. A border should appear around it.

2. Click and drag the chart handles (on the corners and centre of each border edge) to resize the chart area. Drag any corner handle slightly inwards to reduce the chart size.

3. Move the mouse pointer over the chart border, click and hold the mouse button down. Drag the chart around the slide (a faint outline of it should be visible). Release the mouse button.

4. Jean Barker now has an assistant, Use **Add Shape** and **Add Assistant** to add the box then enter the details **Neera Singh, Accounts**.

5. Joanne Malone has left and been replaced by Eileen Dover. Select the text **Joanne Malone** in the box and replace it with **Eileen Dover**.

6. Michael Jones has left and not been replaced. Click on the edge of his shape (make sure there is a solid border) and press <**Delete**>.

7. Click on the edge of the shape for Susan Li (make sure there is a solid border). Right click and select **Cut** from the shortcut menu.

8. Select the Andrew Wilson shape (solid border), right click and select **Paste**. Susan Li is now positioned alongside Andrew Wilson, both reporting to Eileen Dover.

9. With Susan Li's shape still selected, click ⬥ Promote from the **Create Graphic** group. Susan Li is now reporting directly to Brian Brown.

10. Click **Demote** from the **Create Graphic** group and Susan reports to Eileen Dover again.

11. Move the mouse over the available **Layouts** and **SmartArt Styles** on the **Ribbon** to view how the organisation chart could be changed.

12. Select a different **Style**.

13. Click **Reset Graphic** to revert to the original layout.

14. Save the presentation and leave it open.

Driving Lesson 43 - Inserting Images

▣ Park and Read

PowerPoint has a useful **Clip Gallery**, where images and symbols can be chosen for insertion on a presentation slide.

ⓘ *Due to the large number of graphics included with Office 2007, some of them are stored online. If graphics used in the following Driving Lessons are unavailable, replace the specified graphic with an alternative. Graphics from other programs can also be incorporated into presentations - providing that they can be imported.*

ⓘ *As mentioned in an earlier exercise, Office 2007 allows features including Clip Art, to be downloaded from Microsoft directly into PowerPoint. Downloading Clip Art images using a dial up Internet connection 56k or lower may take a long time and therefore it would be advisable that this option should be disabled if you don't have a broadband connection.*

⌒ Manoeuvres

1. Using the presentation from the previous Driving Lesson, view slide **3** in **Normal** view and use the **New Slide** button to insert a new **Title and Content** slide (**4**).

2. Add the slide title **An Example Of Clip Art** and centre it.

3. Click the **Clip Art** icon, ⊞, in the centre of the slide, to add **Clip Art**. The **Clip Art Task Pane** is displayed. The contents of the gallery will vary depending on installation and there may be a delay as the images load.

4. Any picture could be selected or specific searches can be made. Enter **cars** in the **Search for** box and click **Go**. Only pictures that meet the search criteria are displayed.

5. Click on any picture from those displayed.

6. The picture is now inserted on the presentation slide (the **Picture Tools, Format** tab will be displayed).

ⓘ *Clip Art can be added to any slide layout using the Insert tab and selecting the Clip Art button.*

7. Leave the presentation open.

Driving Lesson 44 - Manipulating Images

▣ Park and Read

Images can be copied, moved, resized and deleted

⌒ Manoeuvres

1. The picture will probably already be selected, i.e. have handles visible. If not, click once on it to display the handles.

2. Practise resizing the picture by clicking and dragging on the handles. Click and drag the corner handles to maintain the correct proportions of the picture.

3. Hold down the <**Ctrl**> key and then click and drag one of the handles. This time, the picture is resized about its centre.

4. Practise moving the picture. Hold down the <**Shift**> key as the picture is dragged to <u>move</u> the image either horizontally or vertically.

5. Select the picture and click on the **Copy** button, 🔲, then **Paste**, 🔲, to create another copy of the picture on the same slide. Move them apart.

6. To delete the copied picture, click on it and then press <**Delete**>.

7. To move the original image to another slide, select the image and click on the **Cut** button, ✀.

8. View slide **2** and click on the **Paste** button, 🔲, to place the image on this slide.

9. Delete this slide from the presentation by switching to **Slide Sorter** view and clicking **Delete**, 🔲 Delete.

10. View the third slide in **Normal** view and from the **Slides** group, select **Layout**. Select the **Title Only** layout, change the title to **New Clip Art**.

11. Now click on **Paste** to paste the picture on to this slide.

12. Open the **Garage** presentation and insert a new blank slide and click 🔲 to paste the image to this presentation.

13. Click to paste the image to this presentation.

ℹ *Images can be copied <u>or</u> moved between presentations in this way.*

14. Close the **Garage** presentation <u>without</u> saving and leave the **CIA** presentation open for the next Driving Lesson.

Driving Lesson 45 - Animating Images

Park and Read

Animation effects have been applied to text earlier, but they can also be applied to images.

 Manoeuvres

1. With slide **3** of the presentation on screen select the clip art image by clicking on it.

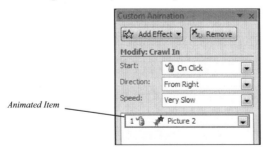

2. To animate the image, select the **Animations** tab and then click the **Custom Animation** button.

3. Click the **Add Effect** button in the **Custom Animation Task Pane** and select the **Entrance** option.

4. Select the **Crawl In** effect (it may be necessary to select **More Effects** and click **OK** first).

5. From the boxes in the **Custom Animation Task Pane** select a direction of **From Right** and a speed of **Very Slow**.

Animated Item

6. Click the **Play** button to see the effect.

7. To change the animation effect, select the **Picture#** from the list, click the **Change** button and make a new selection. Click **Play** to see the effect.

8. To remove animation **1**, select it by clicking on it in the **Custom Animation** task pane and then click **Remove**, Remove. Animation is deleted.

9. Save the presentation and leave it open for the next Driving Lesson.

Driving Lesson 46 - Tables

▣ Park and Read

There are various ways to present data in *PowerPoint*. Tables often provide a clearer way than text to present numerical data.

↱ Manoeuvres

1. Create a new slide at the end of the presentation based on the **Title and Content** slide layout. Enter the title **Sales Table**.

2. Click the **Insert Table** icon in the centre of the slide.

i *Alternatively, use the **Insert Table** button from the **Insert** tab.*

3. From the **Insert Table** dialog box, select **4** columns and **2** rows.

4. Click **OK** and enter the following data into the table, pressing <**Tab**> to move from cell to cell, or <**Shift Tab**> to move back a cell.

Sales Table			
2004	2005	2006	2007
255,000	289,000	364,000	380,000

5. There is more data to add to the table. To insert a new row, click in the second row. From the **Table Tools** section of the **Ribbon**, select the **Layout** tab.

6. From the **Rows and Columns** group, click on the **Insert Above** button.

7. In the new row **2**, enter the following figures: **350,000**, **439,000**, **424,000** and **475,000**.

8. These figures don't make much sense. A column must be inserted at the left. Click in the left column. Select the **Layout** tab again, if not already selected and then click on the **Insert Left** button,

Driving Lesson 46 - Continued

9.   The table should automatically resize to fit the slide.

10. In row **1** of the new column, enter **Year**. Below, enter **Turnover** and on the bottom row, **Profit**.

11. Edit the **2005 Turnover** figure **439,000** to **389,000** by clicking on the cell and making the change.

Sales Table

Year	2004	2005	2006	2007
Turnover	350,000	389,000	424,000	475,000
Profit	255,000	289,000	364,000	380,000

12. Position the cursor just to the left of the first cell in the top row until it becomes a black arrow.

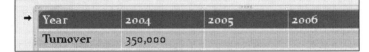

Year	2004	2005	2006
Turnover	350,000		

13. Click to select the whole row. Click the **Center** button from the **Alignment** group. All cells in the row are centred.

14. Position the cursor just above first cell in the top row and click to select the whole column. Click the **Center** button to centre the whole column.

15. Move the cursor over the divider between rows **2** and **3** until it becomes ⬍. Click and drag down to increase the height of the second row until it is around twice its original height. Repeat this for the bottom row.

i *The same method can be used to resize the column widths.*

16. It has been decided that the **2004** column is no longer required. Click in the column and then from the **Layout** tab, click on the **Delete** button, then select **Delete Columns**.

i *Rows are removed in a similar way by selecting the row/s and then the **Delete** button then clicking **Delete Rows**.*

17. There is probably a better way to present data like this. Click on the table border to select the whole table and then press <**Delete**>.

18. Delete the slide and leave the presentation open for the next Driving Lesson.

Driving Lesson 47 - Spreadsheets

▣ Park and Read

Spreadsheets are probably a better way to present data like this. A spreadsheet file can be inserted directly into a presentation.

⌐ Manoeuvres

1. Create a new **Title Only** slide at the end of the presentation.

2. Add the title **Spreadsheet Extract**.

3. To insert data from a spreadsheet, select the **Insert** tab then click on the **Object** button from within the **Text** group.

4. From the **Insert Object** dialog box, select **Create from file** and then click **Browse....**

5. Locate the data files and select the file **Sales.xlsx** (make sure **Files of type** shows **All Files**).

6. Click **OK** and then **OK** in the **Insert Object** dialog box to insert the spreadsheet extract.

7. Make the extract bigger and move it to the centre, so that the slide looks something like the one on the right.

8. Save the presentation and leave it open for the next Driving Lesson.

Spreadsheet Extract

Company Sales			
	North	**Central**	**South**
January	£13,000	£11,743	£9,466
February	£14,376	£10,833	£10,744
March	£14,244	£12,500	£14,775

Driving Lesson 48 - Charts

▣ Park and Read

You can insert charts into a presentation. Sometimes a chart makes figures easier to understand.

↱ Manoeuvres

1. Create a new **Title and Content** slide at the end of the presentation. Close the **Clip Art** and **Custom Animation** task panes, if not already closed and make sure the *PowerPoint* window is maximised.

2. Enter the slide title **Chart** and click on the **Insert Chart** icon on the slide. The **Insert Chart** dialog box is displayed showing the available chart types. Click **OK** to accept the default type of **Clustered Column**.

▣ *A chart can be inserted on to a slide with a different layout by clicking the **Chart** button on the **Insert** tab.*

3. A new spreadsheet window is displayed on the right of the screen showing a sample set of data. The slide with a sample chart, based on the data, is shown on the left.

A6	▾		*fx*	
◢	A	B	C	D
1		Series 1	Series 2	Series 3
2	Category 1	4.3	2.4	2
3	Category 2	2.5	4.4	2
4	Category 3	3.5	1.8	3
5	Category 4	4.5	2.8	5
6				
7				
8		To resize chart data range, drag low		

4. The spreadsheet can be edited to the user's specification by changing figures, titles, etc. Rows and columns can be added or removed. In the spreadsheet, click on **Series 1** and overtype it with **Word**.

5. Replace **Series 2** with **Excel** and **Series 3** with **Access** then press **<Enter>**.

6. Close the datasheet window at the right of the screen using its **Close** button.

7. Leave the **Chart** slide on screen for the next Driving Lesson.

Driving Lesson 49 - Formatting Charts

▣ Park and Read

There are various buttons on the **Design** tab of **Chart Tools**, used for changing the appearance of a chart as well as other methods. This tab will only be available when a chart on a slide is selected. Double clicking on a chart will automatically make this tab active.

☞ Manoeuvres

1. Click on the chart to select it, and make sure the **Chart Tools Design** tab is displayed. Move the mouse around the chart to display **ToolTips,** which indicate the area of the chart beneath. Use this method to locate the **Plot Area**, which is the back wall of the chart.

🛈 *On 3-D charts, the Plot Area is replaced by Back Wall, Side Wall and Floor.*

2. Right clicking on any part of the chart displays a shortcut menu for that area. Right click on the **Plot Area** and select **Format Plot Area**.

3. Select **Picture or texture fill**. Click the **Texture** button, and select **Blue tissue paper**. Click **Close**.

4. Use the **ToolTip** to locate the **Word data series** (any of the data columns for Word). Right click and select **Format Data Series** to display the **Format Data Series** dialog box.

5. Select **Fill** and then **Solid fill**, then click the **Color** button. Select a dark red colour then click **Close**.

6. Right click on the text **Category 1** (horizontal axis). A shortcut menu and a formatting toolbar appear. Use the formatting toolbar to change the font to **Times New Roman** and **Bold Italics**. Click on a blank area of the chart to clear the toolbar from the screen.

7. Click on the **Edit Data** button. The datasheet window is re-opened.

8. Change the **Word** figures for **Category 1** from **4.3** to **5.2**. Press <Enter>. The change is reflected immediately in the chart. Close the data window again.

Driving Lesson 49 - Continued

9. Click **Change Chart Type**, to display the **Change Chart Type** dialog box. From the list at the left, click on each chart type in turn. A list of each chart's sub-types is displayed on the right hand side.

10. Select the **Clustered Bar** under **Bar** chart and click **OK**.

11. Select some different **Chart Styles** from the **Ribbon**, more are available using the drop down arrow. Finally choose **Style 10** (use the **ToolTip** to locate it).

12. Insert another new **Chart** slide at the end of the presentation. Select a **Line chart** (first sub type) and use the default data.

13. Change the slide title to **Line Chart** then close the data window.

14. Create another **Chart** slide at the end of the presentation, this time selecting a **Pie chart** type (second sub type, **Pie in 3-D**) and change the slide title as appropriate. Notice that only one data series is created for the pie chart. Close the data window.

15. Using the methods learnt earlier, change the colour of the **Plot Area** of the **Line chart** to pale green and of the **Pie chart** to lilac.

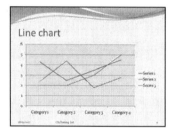   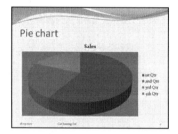

16. On the **Pie chart**, click on the "Pie" itself to select the **Data Series**, then click again on a single slice to select the individual **Data Point**. Right click and select **Format Data Point**.

17. Select **Fill** and then **Solid fill**, then click the **Color** button. Select yellow then click **Close**. The colour of one slice is changed.

18. From the **Slides pane** in **Normal** view, click on the **Bar chart** slide to select it and then hold down the <**Shift**> key.

19. Still holding down <**Shift**>, click on the **Pie chart** slide. The three chart slides are now selected. To delete these new slides, press <**Delete**>.

20. Save the changes to the presentation and leave it open for the next Driving Lesson.

Driving Lesson 50 - Adding Chart Labels

Park and Read

Titles can be added to charts to identify specific areas. You can also add data labels to show actual precise values or percentages for each data series in the chart (only Pie charts can show percentages).

Manoeuvres

1. At the end of the presentation insert a new **Title and Content** slide with the title **Chart**, and click the icon to add a chart.

2. Select the second **Bar chart** sub type **Stacked Bar**. Click **OK** and close the data window.

3. Select the chart then the **Layout** tab from the **Chart Tools** section of the **Ribbon**. Click the **Data Labels** button from the **Labels** group then from the drop down list, select the **Inside End** option.

4. Add a chart title by selecting **Chart Title** from the **Labels** group, choose the **Above Chart** option from the list.

5. When the title then appears, change it to **UK Regions**.

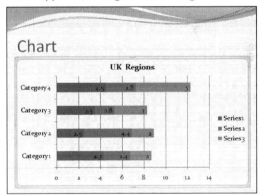

6. Right click on the chart and select **Change Chart Type** from the options.

7. Select the first **Pie** chart type and click **OK**.

8. Right click on one of the pie segments and select **Format Data Labels**.

9. Select **Label Options** from the left panel. Click **Value** to remove the values, and click **Percentage** to add percentage labels. Click **Close** to see the effect.

10. Save the presentation and leave it open for the next Driving Lesson.

Driving Lesson 51 - Drawing & Objects

Park and Read

The **Shapes** tools from the **Drawing** group allow drawings to be made directly on to a slide. The tools can only be displayed in **Normal** view and **Notes Pages** view. The buttons relating to drawing are all available from the **Shapes** button.

Objects can be drawn by clicking on the appropriate button and then clicking and dragging on the slide. All objects have **handles**, similar to clip art, that can be used to reshape and re-size the drawing.

Manoeuvres

1. Using the **CIA** presentation, create a new, **Title Only**, slide after the existing slides and enter the title **Drawing**.

2. Select the **Home** tab and locate the **Drawing** group.

3. Click **Shapes**, , to reveal the available shapes that can be drawn.

4. From **Lines**, click the **Line** button, ⬚, then click and drag a line on the slide.

5. In a similar way, draw a rectangle anywhere on the slide.

6. To draw a freeform line, from **Lines**, click **Freeform**, ⬚. Click and hold down the mouse and drag to create a curving line.

7. Double click to complete the freeform line.

8. Draw a block arrow from **AutoShapes**.

9. Practise drawing lines, rectangles, squares, arrows, circles and ovals (ellipses).

ℹ️ *Holding down <Shift> while drawing an oval will create a circle or, while drawing a rectangle, will produce a square.*

Driving Lesson 52 - Formatting Drawn Objects

▣ Park and Read

The buttons located within the **Format** tab which appears on the **Ribbon** when a drawn object is selected allow changes to be made. Objects are selected by clicking on them, when selected they then display their handles.

⌐ Manoeuvres

1. Click on an oval, drawn in the previous exercise to select it. It displays its handles, the **Format** tab is also displayed in the **Ribbon**.

2. Click on the drop down arrow on the **Shape Fill** button, [Shape Fill ▾]. Choose a different colour from the options.

3. Change the line colour by clicking on the drop down arrow on the **Shape Outline** button, [Shape Outline ▾] and selecting a colour.

4. Now select a rectangle, then click the **Shape Effects** button, [Shape Effects ▾]. Select **Shadow**.

5. From the grid displayed, use **Tooltips** to find **Offset Left**. Click the button to apply the shadow.

6. Move the rectangle - the shadow moves with it.

7. Click **Shapes** and select the **Text Box** tool from **Basic Shapes**.

8. Click and drag with the tool to draw a small rectangular text box. The typing cursor will be flashing at the left of the box.

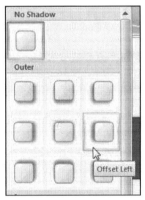

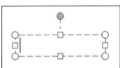

9. Type the text **Special Offer - Today Only**. The box will enlarge to take the text if necessary.

10. Click on one of the previously drawn lines and change its thickness by clicking [Shape Outline ▾], selecting **Weight** and choosing from the one of the options.

Driving Lesson 52 - Continued

11. With the line still selected, click and drag to move it around on the slide.

12. Change the line to an arrow by first selecting it and then clicking [Shape Outline ▾], and then **Arrows**.

13. Choose the **Double Ended Arrow** option.

14. The start and end style of arrows can be changed. Make sure the arrow line is selected and click [Shape Outline ▾], select **Arrows** and then **More Arrows**.

15. From **End type** within the **Arrows** area, choose the **Oval Arrow**.

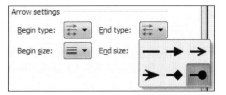

16. Click **Close** to apply the style to the arrow.

17. Right click on a square and select **Edit Text** from the shortcut menu. A cursor flashes in the shape.

18. Type your first name into the square. Click outside the shape to complete the process

19. In the same way, add your name to a block arrow, a rectangle, an oval and a circle.

20. Leave the presentation open for the next Driving Lesson.

Driving Lesson 53 - Rotate or Flip Objects

▣ Park and Read

Any drawn object can be rotated or flipped.

↻ Manoeuvres

1. Using the **Drawing** slide, click on the **Shapes** button. (or **Insert Shapes** if the **Drawing Tools** is open)

2. Click on the **Heart** shape from **Basic Shapes**, then click and drag on the slide to draw a heart. As well as the white sizing handles each object has a green **Rotate** handle.

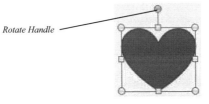

Rotate Handle

3. Move the mouse pointer over the **Rotate** handle of the heart. The cursor changes to [icon]. Click and drag. The object rotates about the centre.

4. Try rotating the object whilst holding down <**Shift**>. The object rotates in fixed steps.

5. Select or draw an oval.

6. Rotate the oval so it is at an angle, like in the diagram below:

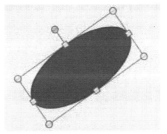

7. To flip the oval, click the **Format** tab. From the **Arrange** group, click **Rotate**, [Rotate icon] and select **Flip Vertical**.

8. Try rotating and flipping some other objects. Flipping symmetrical objects such as circles and squares will not produce any visible effects. Leave the presentation open for the next Driving Lesson.

Driving Lesson 54 - Manipulating Objects

▣ Park and Read

Click and drag an object to move it around a slide, or cut and paste it to move it between slides, or to a different presentation. Click and drag the handles of any object to change its size. Objects can also be copied within a presentation or to another one. Handles on a chart are shown as dots within its border.

℞ Manoeuvres

1. Move to the **Chart** slide and click once on the chart to select it. To resize the chart, move over the top right handle until the cursor changes, ⬚. Click and drag inwards to reduce the size of the chart.

2. Use the same handle to click and drag outward until the chart is slightly larger but not filling the slide.

3. Move over the border of the chart until the cursor changes, ⬚ and drag it to a new position on the slide.

4. Move it back to its original position.

5. With the chart still selected, click ✂ to remove it. Open the **Marketing** presentation and create a new **Blank** slide at the end.

6. To move the chart to this presentation, click ⬚.

7. The chart should be selected, if not click on it once. Press <**Delete**> to delete it.

8. Use the **Taskbar** to move to the **CIA** presentation and the **Chart** slide, then click ⬚ to replace the chart in its original position.

9. Now click ⬚ to duplicate the chart (notice the original is untouched).

10. Create a new blank slide at the end of the presentation and click **Paste** to copy the chart here.

Driving Lesson 54 - Continued

11. Move back to the **Marketing** presentation and select the last slide.

12. Paste the chart again on the blank slide. Delete it and move back to the **CIA** presentation.

13. Select the **Drawing** slide and select any square/rectangle. Resizing and moving is the same for all objects. Click and drag a corner handle outward to make the object bigger.

14. With the object selected, click the **Cut** button, , and move to the **Marketing** presentation. Click to paste the drawn object.

15. Select and then delete the object in the same way as deleting a chart.

16. Move back to the **CIA** presentation and the **Drawing** slide. Select any drawn object.

17. Copy it, then paste it into the blank slide at the end of the **Marketing** presentation. Use the **Smart tag** to **Keep Source Formatting**.

18. Close the **Marketing** presentation <u>without</u> saving and leave the **CIA** presentation open.

Driving Lesson 55 - Arranging Objects

▣ Park and Read

Objects on a slide can be thought of as pieces of overlaying paper; they sometimes overlap, covering important information. The order of objects can be changed if necessary, by moving them backward or forward.

☞ Manoeuvres

1. Using the **Drawing** slide, click on any object. Press **<Shift>** and select another object. Both objects should now be selected and any formatting will be applied to both objects. Click and drag a corner handle on one of the objects, both objects will be equally resized. Click away to deselect them.

2. From the **Editing** group, click on **Select** and then **Selection Pane**.

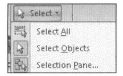

3. From this pane, select one of the object names. Notice how the handles appear. Hold down **<Ctrl>** and click on another object name, in the pane. Handles will appear on that object too.

4. Move one shape slightly to the left - all of the selected objects move. Click away from the objects to deselect them.

5. Arrange several of the objects on the slide so that they are **on top** of each other.

6. Select the object that is on top of the others. Select the **Format** tab. Click the drop down arrow on **Send to Back**, [Send to Back ▾]

Driving Lesson 55 - Continued

7.   Select **Send to Back** from the list displayed. The object will now be **under** the others.

8.   Click 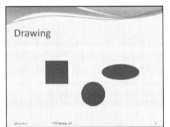 to bring the object back to the top.

9.   Practise using the **Back/Front** and **Forward/Backward** options within **Arrange** to rearrange objects. Notice the difference between bringing an object <u>forward</u> and bringing it to the <u>front</u>.

10. Delete all objects on the slide and draw a square, a circle and an oval. Move them to random positions similar to that shown below.

11. To align the objects to the top of the slide, first select them all.

12. Display the **Format** tab. From **Arrange** click ⊨ Align ▾ make sure that **Align to Slide** is selected.

13. Select **Align Top** from the **Align** options. All the objects are aligned with the top of the slide.

ℹ️ *If **Align to Slide** had not been selected, the objects would be aligned with the top edge of the highest of the objects.*

14. To align the objects to the right, select **Align** and then **Align Right**. The objects are now on top of each other because they have not been distributed.

15. From **Align**, select **Distribute Vertically**. The objects are distributed evenly over the vertical edge of the slide.

16. Use the **Align** button to align the objects to the left of the slide.

17. Now align them at the bottom of the slide and then distribute them horizontally.

18. Finally, use **Align Middle** to line up the objects across the middle of the slide.

ℹ️ *Any objects, i.e. drawn objects, **Clip Art** pictures, or images from file can be manipulated in this way.*

19. Click away from the objects to deselect them and leave the slide on screen.

Driving Lesson 56 - Grouping Objects

▣ Park and Read

Objects can be grouped; this allows them to be treated as a single object.

⌒ Manoeuvres

1. Click on the object at the left. To group the objects, hold down **<Shift>** and click on the others in turn.

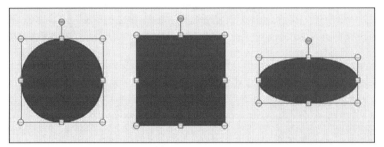

2. Click on the **Arrange** button on the **Home** tab and select **Group** from the drop down menu, as on the right.

3. Try moving one object - notice how they all move.

4. Use the single green rotate handle to rotate the grouped objects, see what happens.

5. Rotate the group back to their original position.

6. Click on the **Arrange** button again and then select **Ungroup**, ⊡ Ungroup, to separate the objects. They can now be manipulated individually once again.

7. Deselect the objects.

8. Leave the slide on screen.

Driving Lesson 57 - Colours and Lines

▣ Park and Read

Drawn objects (including text boxes) can have the colour of their lines and fills changed. The style of the line may also be changed.

↱ Manoeuvres

1. To begin changing the lines and fill colours, double click on the object to be formatted. Using the **Drawing** slide from the previous Driving Lesson, double click on any of the objects on the slide.

2. The **Format** tab appears. Click on **Shape Fill**. **Theme Colors** suggest colours that are associated with this colour scheme. Select a green.

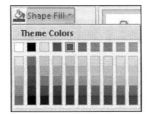

3. From the **Shape Fill** option, select **More Fill Colors**.

4. Change the **Transparency** setting to **50%**, ether by using the slider or the value box, then click **OK**. Move the object over the title, **Drawing** - the text should be visible underneath the shape.

Transparency: ◄   ►   50 % ⬍

5. Drag the object away from the title and click **Shape Fill**.

6. Select **Texture** and view the various effects available before choosing one of the available **Texture** options.

7. Change the shape outline, colour, weight and dash effects using options from ⬚ Shape Outline ▾.

8. Leave the presentation on screen for the next Driving Lesson.

Driving Lesson 58 - Importing Images

▣ Park and Read

Images can be imported into *PowerPoint* from other files.

⌐ Manoeuvres

1. Using the presentation **CIA**, create a new blank slide at the end of the presentation ready to accept an imported picture.

2. To import an image from a file, select **Insert** tab and click **Picture** to display the **Insert Picture** dialog box.

3. The file called **CIA Logo** can be found in **C:\Documents\CIA DATA FILES\ECDL\6 Presentations**, click on the name.

ℹ️ The **Insert Picture** dialog box can appear in many different views, which can be selected using the **Views** button, 🔲 **Views** ▾. The view shown here is **Small Icons**.

4. Click **Insert**.

5. The image will be placed on the new slide and can then be enlarged and repositioned by clicking and dragging, the same as any other object.

6. Save the presentation and close it.

Driving Lesson 59 - Revision

This covers the features introduced in this section. Try not to refer to the preceding Driving Lessons while completing it.

1.   Using a new, blank presentation, create a new slide based on an organisation chart, with the title **Little Town F.C.**.

2.   Create the chart below:

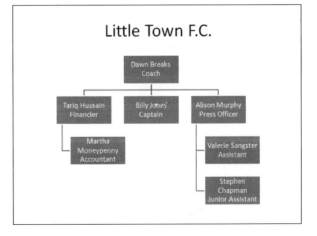

3.   Now modify it to produce this chart layout:

Driving Lesson 59 - Continued

4. Create a new blank slide.

5. Insert a picture from the **Clip Gallery**.

6. Place it on the slide. Insert a second image.

7. **Copy** and **paste** one of the images, within the same slide.

8. **Resize** one of the images.

9. Create another new slide containing a **Chart**.

10. Give it the title **My Chart** and using the information in the default data, create a **pie chart**.

11. This chart is not appropriate for the data. Change the chart type to a **3-D Clustered Column**.

12. Change the colour of the chart walls (**Walls**) to light blue and the area around the chart (**Plot Area**) to green.

13. Change the colour of the data series to any colour scheme desired.

14. On a new blank slide import the image with the filename **Pyramid**. Re-size as required.

15. Create another new blank slide and produce some drawings using the **Shapes** tools.

16. Save the presentation as **Examples** and close it.

If you experienced any difficulty completing the Revision, refer back to the Driving Lessons in this section. Then redo the Revision.

Driving Lesson 60 - Revision

This covers the features introduced in this section. Try not to refer to the preceding Driving Lessons while completing it.

1. Create a new blank presentation and set the first slide to have the **Title and Content** layout.

2. Insert the title **Victoria's Wine Sales - Table**.

3. Insert a table with **5** columns & **4** rows.

4. Enter the information shown below into the table. Use the <**Tab**> key to move to the next cell when the data for a cell has been entered. Use <**Tab**> with <**Shift**> held down to move back one cell. Click in any cell to edit the data there:

	January	February	March	Total
Red	120	112	142	**374**
White	280	247	228	**755**
Rose	98	90	87	**275**

5. Change table style to achieve an appearance similar to that above.

6. Insert a column for **April** in the appropriate place. Enter the following figures: **Red 172**, **White 250**, **Rose 103**.

7. Correct the totals (546, 1005, 378)

8. Create a new **Title and Content** slide, where a column chart is to be created. Enter the title **Victoria's Wine Sales - Chart**.

9. Using the data in the table from the previous slide, retype the figures into the datasheet, to make a column chart. **Category 1** is **January**, **2** is **February**, **3** is **March** and **4** is **April**. **Series 1** is **Red**, **2** is **White** and **3** is **Rosé**. Do not include the **Total** column.

10. Add data labels showing **values**.

11. Close the data sheet.

12. Save the presentation as **Wine Sales**.

13. Close the presentation.

If you experienced any difficulty completing the Revision, refer back to the Driving Lessons in this section. Then redo the Revision.

Driving Lesson 61 - Revision

This covers the features introduced in this section. Try not to refer to the preceding Driving Lessons while completing it.

1. Create a new presentation using the **Concourse Theme**. Change the slide layout to **Title Only**. Change the **Background Style** to **Style 2**.

2. Add the title **Office Layout**.

3. Draw a large rectangle underneath the title and change the fill colour to represent the floor.

4. Draw a filled oval that surrounds the title, but place it in the background so that the text can be seen.

5. Change the fill colour of the oval to dark blue.

6. Change the text colour to white.

7. Use the **Clip Art** keyword search **shapes** to reveal many small clip art images, including some which can be used for creating room layouts.

8. Create an office layout according to the following instructions. Moving, rotating and resizing of objects will be required.

9. Place a desk along the west (left) wall of the office.

10. Place a chair next to the desk.

11. Insert a 3-seater couch and a circular table and place in the top right hand corner of the room.

12. Add a door swing in the middle of the south wall of the room and a file cabinet in the middle of the north wall.

13. Insert a plant on the round table and a telephone and PC on the desk.

14. Select the rectangle representing the floor and add a **3pt** black line.

15. Save the presentation as **Layout**.

16. Close the presentation.

i *An example Office Layout is shown in the Answers at the back of the guide.*

If you experienced any difficulty completing the Revision, refer back to the Driving Lessons in this section. Then redo the Revision.

Once you are confident with the features, complete the Record of Achievement Matrix referring to the section at the end of the guide. Only when competent move on to the next Section.

Section 5
Slide Shows

By the end of this Section you should be able to:

Select the Correct Output Format

Set up a Slide Show

Apply Slide Transitions

Run the Presentation

Print Slides, Presentations and Handouts

To gain an understanding of the above features, work through the **Driving Lessons** in this **Section**.

For each **Driving Lesson**, read the **Park and Read** instructions, without touching the keyboard, then work through the numbered steps of the **Manoeuvres** on the computer. Complete the **Revision Exercise(s)** at the end of the section to test your knowledge.

Driving Lesson 62 - Output Format

▣ Park and Read

A presentation can be given using different methods, such as on an overhead projector, an on-screen show, or just as handouts for the audience. The output format should be selected before the presentation is run.

↱ Manoeuvres

1. Open the presentation **Hospital**. The presentation is to be shown on an overhead projector. Select the **Design** tab and click **Page Setup**.

2. The presentation is currently set up as an **On-screen Show**. Click on the drop down list for **Slides sized for**.

    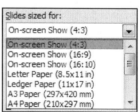

3. Select **Overhead** and click **OK**.

4. Click **Page Setup** and change the slides size setting to **A4 Paper** and click **OK**. This would print one slide per sheet.

5. From the **Page Setup** dialog box, change the size to **Letter Paper**.

6. Click **OK**. The slide image changes slightly to indicate how it would look when printed on **Letter** size paper.

7. From the **Page Setup** dialog box, select the **Custom** size option. The size of the slide can now be defined using the **Height** and **Width** boxes. Set a height of **20cm** and a width of **10cm** and click **OK** to see the effect.

8. Now change the format back to **On-screen show (4:3)** and **Slide Orientation** to **Landscape**. Click **OK**. Leave the presentation open.

Driving Lesson 63 - Slide Setup

🅿 Park and Read

The slide setup, e.g. the slide orientation may be changed, as well as the orientation of the **Notes Pages**, **Handouts** and **Outlines**.

🏳 Manoeuvres

1. Using the presentation **Hospital**, with the first slide in **Normal** view, click on the **Design** tab.

2. To change the orientation of the slides in the presentation, click **Slide Orientation**.

3. Select **Portrait**. The slide orientation changes.

Landscape   *Portrait*

ℹ️ *Within the **Page Setup** dialog box, which can be displayed by clicking the **Page Setup** button on the **Design** tab, there is also an option to separately change the orientation of the **Notes, handouts and outline** pages, illustrated below.*

4. Run the show. The slide does not fill the screen, so, while this might be useful in some circumstances, it is not here.

5. Return the slide orientation to **Landscape**.

Driving Lesson 64 - Setting up a Slide Show

🅿 Park and Read

The following Driving Lessons demonstrate how to set up and run a slide show, with transitions and timings, etc.

☞ Manoeuvres

1. With the **Hospital** presentation open and the **Slide** pane on the left, select the **Slide Show** tab and click **Set Up Slide Show**. The **Set Up Show** dialog box appears.

2. Make selections in the dialog box opting for **Show type** set to **Presented by a speaker**, **Show slides** set to **All** and **Advance slides** set to **Manually**.

Show type	Show slides
⦿ Presented by a speaker (full screen)	⦿ All
○ Browsed by an individual (window)	○ From: [ ] To: [ ]
☐ Show scrollbar	○ Custom show:
○ Browsed at a kiosk (full screen)	[▾]

ℹ️ *Note there is an option under **Show slides** to start and end the slide show with specific slides, e.g. from slide 2 to slide 6.*

3. Click **OK**.

4. Click [From Beginning] to start the slide show with the first slide in the presentation. Note this is not necessarily slide 1 if a range of slides had been specified in **Show slides**.

5. Click the mouse to move to the second slide. Change the mouse pointer to the **Ballpoint Pen** using the **Pointer Options** menu. Use the pen to draw on this slide. Change the pointer back to arrow.

6. Move through the rest of the slide show and at the end, click to exit, opting to keep annotations and return to **Normal** view.

7. Select slide 3 of the presentation and click . The show will run again but the first slide shown will be slide 3.

8. Run through the show and end it as before.

9. Leave the presentation open.

Driving Lesson 65 - Slide Transition

Park and Read

A **transition** is a special effect that controls how one slide changes to the next. It refers to the whole slide whereas **animation** applies to the individual text or objects on a slide.

Manoeuvres

1. In **Normal** view, click on the **Title** slide of the **Hospital** presentation.

2. Select the **Animations** tab. The **Transition to This Slide** group is displayed.

3. Hover the mouse over any effect. A demonstration of the effect is shown.

4. Try using some of the other effects from the drop down list to see what they do.

5. Select the effect **Newsflash**, [image], select the speed **Medium**, select some sound if required and make sure the **On Mouse Click** box is checked. The **Title** slide now has its transition effect defined and has a star symbol next to it in the **Slides** pane to indicate this.

6. Click on the second slide and choose a different transition from the list.

7. Apply transition effects to the rest of the slides (use **Apply to All** if the same transitions are to be used on each slide).

> **i** *To remove a transition, select the **No Transition** button from the Ribbon.*

8. Select the first slide then click on the **Slide Show** button to run the slide show. Click the mouse button to move from one slide to the next.

9. Select the first slide in **Slide Sorter** view.

10. To change the transition, select the **Wedge** effect, [image], from the **Transition to This Slide** group with a **Medium** speed and select to **Apply to All**.

11. Run the slide show to see the new effects.

12. Save the presentation as **Transitions** and close it.

Driving Lesson 66 - The Presentation

Park and Read

Assume that the **CIA Training Ltd**. presentation is now complete. All that remains now is to practise slide navigation and then to print the slides, handouts and notes, etc.

Manoeuvres

1. Open the **CIA** presentation and display the **Slide Show** tab.

2. The slides in the presentation are to be advanced manually using the mouse button. Click the **Set Up Slide Show** button.

3. Make sure the settings in the **Set Up Show** dialog box are set so that the slides are advanced manually and timings are disabled.

4. The **Slide Show** button, 🖳, in the lower right of the window, starts the slide show from the currently selected slide. To start the presentation with the third slide, select slide 3 before clicking 🖳 to start the slide show.

5. Press <**Esc**> to end the show. Slide **5** is not to be viewed during this presentation, hide it by selecting the slide first and then clicking on **Hide Slide** from the **Set Up** group. Notice the icon in the **Slides** pane, 🖳.

6. Run the show from slide **1** and notice that slide **5** will not appear.

7. To view slide **5** in future presentations, select the slide, then click **Hide Slide** to switch off the feature.

8. Run the show again from slide **1**, but do not move on.

9. Move the mouse pointer to the bottom left hand corner of the slide to reveal the **popup menu**.

Slide navigation arrows

Arrow and highlighting options   *Navigation menu*

10. Click the navigation menu. View the slide options and select **Go to Slide**.

11. Select the slide **5**. The show will jump to that slide.

12. Display the popup menu again, and explore the other options.

13. Exit the show by pressing <**Esc**> and leave the presentation open.

Driving Lesson 67 - Printing

🅿 Park and Read

In *PowerPoint* you can print out slides, notes pages, outlines and handouts in various formats. When printing slides, there is the choice of whether to print **All** the slides, just the **Current** slide or just the specified **Slides**.

Manoeuvres

ℹ️ *To preview the slides before printing, select the **Office Button**, scroll down to **Print**, then select **Print Preview**.*

1. In any view, click the **Office Button** and select **Print** or use the key press **<Ctrl P>**. The **Print** dialog box is displayed. The **Preview** button, Preview , in the dialog box can be used to preview any print selection before printing. Using this instead of printing will save paper.

Driving Lesson 67 - Continued

2. From **Print what**, select **Slides**. From **Copies** and **Print range** respectively, opt to print **1** copy of **All** slides, then click **OK** (or **Preview**).

3. Select slide **1**. Select the **Office Button** and **Print**. From **Print range** select **Current slide**. Select **2** from **Number of copies** and click **OK**. This prints two copies of one slide.

4. To print slides 2 to 4 only: from **Print range** select **Slides,** type **2-4** in the **Slides** box, click **OK**.

5. In the **Print** dialog box, from **Print what** select **Handouts**. The **Handouts** section of the dialog box becomes active. Set **Slides per page** to **3** and click **OK**.

6. Within the **Print** dialog box, use the **Print what** box to print **Notes Pages**. This produces one slide per page with notes for each slide underneath.

7. Within the **Print** dialog box, use the **Print what** box to print **Outline View**. This produces a list of all the text content of the slides.

i

*If you do not have access to a printer, any print of the presentation can be printed to a file instead. Check **Print to file** in the **Print** dialog box. Click **OK** and enter a **File name** in the **Print to File** dialog box. Click **Save**.*

8. Close the presentation, saving the changes.

Driving Lesson 68 - Revision

This covers the features introduced in this section. Try not to refer to the preceding Driving Lessons while completing it.

1. Open the presentation **Gardens**.

2. Apply a theme of your choice to the slides.

3. Change the orientation to **portrait**.

4. Set up and run the slide show.

5. Apply a <u>different</u> transition to <u>each</u> slide.

6. Print one of the slides.

7. Start the presentation on the second slide, with the last slide hidden.

8. Save the presentation as **Gardens2** and close it.

9. Open the presentation **Kittens**.

10. Apply a <u>different</u> transition effect to <u>each</u> of the slides.

11. Run the slide show.

12. Print out the current slide.

13. Print out handouts showing **4** slides per page.

14. Save the presentation as **Cats**.

15. Close the presentation.

16. Close *PowerPoint*.

If you experienced any difficulty completing the Revision, refer back to the Driving Lessons in this section. Then redo the Revision.

Once you are confident with the features, complete the Record of Achievement Matrix referring to the section at the end of the guide.

Answers

Driving Lesson 9

Step 2   **Blank and recent, Installed Templates, Installed Themes, My templates, New from existing** and **Microsoft Office Online.**

Step 3   **3** by default.

Step 4   **Save, Can't Undo** and **Repeat New.**

Step 5   Not available to use at present.

Step 6   The **Ribbon** contains groups of buttons which are used to access the most common commands.

Step 7   The **Review** tab.

Step 8   **Classic Photo Album, Introducing PowerPoint 2007, Contemporary Photo Album, Pitchbook, Quiz Show** and **Widescreen Presentation.**

Step 9   Preferences are basic option settings.

Step 19   **3 - Start Slide Show, Set Up** and **Monitors.**

Driving Lesson 10

Step 4   a) **New Slide**

b) **Format Painter**

c) **Text Shadow**

d) **Save**

e) **Bullets**

f) **Microsoft Office PowerPoint Help**

Driving Lesson 61

Glossary

Alignment	The arrangement of text or objects in relation to the slide or text box, e.g. left, centre, right, top, bottom.
Animation	Special effects which make text and other objects appear to move on screen.
Animation Scheme	A collection of animation effects which can be applied to a slide with a single selection.
Arrange	Position overlapping objects in relation to each other. They can be brought forward or sent backward, placed on the top or bottom of the pile.
Background	The colour of the slide.
Copy	Create a duplicate of an object or text. Used when the copied item is to be duplicated.
Custom Animation	Applying animation effects to individual objects on a slide and specifying their operation.
Cut	Remove an object or text. Used when the cut item is to be moved somewhere else.
Flip	Move an object as if it is reflected, e.g. left becomes right, or top becomes bottom.
Footer	Text or numbers appearing at the bottom of the slide, notes page or handout.
Formatting	Changing the appearance of text, graphics, etc.
Header	Text or numbers appearing at the top of the slide, notes page or handout.
Import	Bring a file into a presentation from another application.
Object	Item on a slide, e.g. drawn shape, image, chart, text box, table.
Orientation	Which way up the slide/handout is: **Portrait** or **Landscape**.
Output Format	How the presentation is to be given, e.g. on screen or using an overhead projector.
Page Setup	Allows the size and orientation of slides to be changed.
Paste	Used after **Cut** or **Copy** to position the item (move or duplicate).
PowerPoint Options	Basic program settings, which can be changed.

Presentation	A collection of slides used by a speaker as a visual aid.
Rotate	Move an object clockwise or anticlockwise about its axis.
Save	Keep a permanent copy of your work on the hard or floppy drive of the computer.
Slide Layout	The type of slide, e.g. **Bulleted List**, **Title Only**, **Chart and Text**, etc.
Slide Master	This view is for adding items that are to appear on all slides in a presentation.
Slides	Make up the presentation, each refers to a specific area.
Slide Show	A preview of the presentation, with all effects, sounds, etc.
Tabs	Contain buttons (icons) in groups to perform tasks quickly.
Text Effects	Formatting such as bold, italic, shadow, superscript.
Themes	*PowerPoint* contains many of these pre-set designs for slides. Applied to all slides.
Transition	How one slide moves to the next.
Views	Different ways of looking at slides.

Index

Record of Achievement Matrix

This Matrix is to be used to measure your progress while working through the guide. This is a learning reinforcement process; you judge when you are competent.

Tick boxes are provided for each feature. 1 is for no knowledge, 2 some knowledge and 3 is for competent. A section is only complete when column 3 is completed for all parts of the section.

For details on sitting ECDL Examinations in your country please contact the local ECDL Licensee or visit the European Computer Driving Licence Foundation Limited web site at http://www.ecdl.org.

Tick the Relevant Boxes **1**: No Knowledge   **2**: Some Knowledge   **3**: Competent

Section	No	Driving Lesson	1	2	3
1 Getting Started	1	Starting PowerPoint			
	2	The PowerPoint Screen			
	3	Presentations			
	4	The Ribbon			
	5	The Quick Access Toolbar			
	6	Help			
	7	Preferences			
	8	Closing PowerPoint			
2 Slides & Presentations	11	Views			
	12	Slide View			
	13	Slides and Outline View			
	14	Slide Sorter View			
	15	Notes Page View			
	16	Slide Show			
	17	Saving a Presentation			
	18	Closing a Presentation			
	19	Opening Presentations			
	20	New Presentations			
	21	Creating a Presentation			
	22	Adding and Deleting Slides			
	23	Changing Slide Layout			
	24	Background Colour			
3 Formatting	27	Formatting: Font & Size			
	28	Undo and Redo			
	29	Applying Text Effects			
	30	Alignment, Spacing & Case			
	31	Bullets			
	32	Cut & Paste			
	33	Copy & Paste			

Tick the Relevant Boxes 1: No Knowledge   2: Some Knowledge   3: Competent

Section	No	Driving Lesson	1	2	3
3 Formatting (continued)	34	Standard Animation			
	35	Custom Animation			
	36	Spell Checking			
	37	Master Pages			
	38	Headers & Footers			
4 PowerPoint Objects	41	Organisation Charts			
	42	Modify Organisation Chart			
	43	Inserting Images			
	44	Manipulating Images			
	45	Animating Images			
	46	Tables			
	47	Spreadsheets			
	48	Charts			
	49	Formatting Charts			
	50	Adding Chart Labels			
	51	Drawing & Objects			
	52	Formatting Drawn Objects			
	53	Rotate or Flip Objects			
	54	Manipulating Objects			
	55	Arranging Objects			
	56	Grouping Objects			
	57	Colours and Lines			
	58	Importing Images			
5 Slide Shows	62	Output Format			
	63	Slide Setup			
	64	Setting Up a Slide Show			
	65	Slide Transition			
	66	The Presentation			
	67	Printing			

Other Products from CiA Training Ltd

CiA Training Ltd is a leading publishing company, which has consistently delivered the highest quality products since 1985. A wide range of flexible and easy to use self teach resources has been developed by CiA's experienced publishing team to aid the learning process. These include the following ECDL Foundation approved products at the time of publication of this product:

- **ECDL/ICDL Syllabus 5.0**

- **ECDL/ICDL Advanced Syllabus 2.0**

- **ECDL/ICDL Revision Series**

- **ECDL/ICDL Advanced Syllabus 2.0 Revision Series**

- **e-Citizen**

Previous syllabus versions also available - contact us for further details.

We hope you have enjoyed using our materials and would love to hear your opinions about them. If you'd like to give us some feedback, please go to:

www.ciatraining.co.uk/feedback.php

and let us know what you think.

New products are constantly being developed. For up to the minute information on our products, to view our full range, to find out more, or to be added to our mailing list, visit:

www.ciatraining.co.uk